AF652240

# INDIA AND RUSSIA

# INDIA AND RUSSIA

## Deepening the Strategic Partnership

*Edited by*
Rajiv K. Bhatia
Vijay Sakhuja
Indrani Talukdar

SHIPRA

INDIAN COUNCIL OF WORLD AFFAIRS

All rights reserved. No part of this publication may be reproduced, stored in a retrieval system, or transmitted in any form or by any means, electronic, mechanical, photocopying, recording or otherwise, without the prior written permission of the Publisher.
The views expressed in this volume are of individual contributor and do not represent the viewpoint of the editors or the Council.

ISBN: 978-81-7541-721-2

First Published in India in 2014

*India and Russia: Deepening the Strategic Partnership*

© Indian Council of World Affairs

*Published by:*
**SHIPRA PUBLICATIONS**
H.O.: LG 18-19, Pankaj Central Market, Patparganj,
I.P. Ext., Delhi-110092, Tel: 91-11-2223 5152, 2223 6152
Br.Off.: 4617/18, Ansari Road, Darya Ganj,
New Delhi-110002, Tel: 9650028065, 9810522367
E-mail: info@shiprapublications.com
www.shiprapublications.com

# Preface

In the larger context of rapidly changing strategic environment, and the historical backdrop of convergences trumping divergences that mark India-Russia bilateral relations, it is important to understand contemporary geo-political and geo-economic scenarios; India-Russia partnership in the multilateral fora; regional issues, especially those affecting the regions that are of immense interest to both the countries; and finally the characteristics, constraints and prospects of the bilateral relations.

India views Russia as an important world player that has wider international influence and responsibility. Indian leadership considers relations with Russia as 'a key pillar' of India's foreign policy. Hence, friendly and cooperative equations between the two countries have vital global and regional significance.

India's worldview encompasses several key elements. Among them figure a commitment to peace and security as essential pre-requisites for economic development—the real priority; reliance on peaceful means and negotiations to resolve inter-state differences; belief that the contemporary world is essentially multi-polar where poles (or pillars) are of varying size and strength and that a working equilibrium among them is crucial for peace and security; and conviction that the world's governance structures should be more representative of shifts in power equations since the end of the Cold War.

Russia's worldview has changed considerably from the times of the USSR. It has factored in changes in the balance of power in the post-Cold War era; it accords primacy to national interests rather than ideology; and it recognizes that 'the bloc-based approach' for tackling international issues is being replaced by 'network diplomacy.' The Soviet Union of the yore was one of the two super powers, whereas Russia today is a significant member of G-8 as well as BRICS.

As evident from the document entitled 'Concept of the Foreign Policy of the Russian Federation' (issued in February 2013 with the approval of President Valdimir Putin), Russia aims to ensure its national security, create favourable external conditions for a steady and dynamic growth of the Russian economy, promote international peace and 'universal security', and develop mutually beneficial and equal bilateral and multilateral partnership relations with foreign states. It is recognized in Moscow that an intense competition is now taking place, 'for the first time in modern history', on a global level, denoting that various models of development tend 'to clash and compete each other.' Besides, for tackling challenges it faces, the world seems to need both joint efforts by the international community based on 'the central coordinating role of the UN' as well as effective, regional governance based on 'the polycentric model' of the world. The latter entails emergence of networks, associations and economic agreements as 'instruments to enhance security and financial and economic stability.' Among various tools at Russia's disposal is public diplomacy which it uses to ensure 'its objective perception in the world.'

A further step in enhancing mutual understanding between India and Russia may be to examine (i) Russia's view of India's role, and (ii) India's view of Russia's role in world affairs.

On the former aspect, a premier Russian Think Tank (RIAC) has recently noted that 'alongside the US and China' India has a rightful claim 'to the status of being a centre of global influence,' but it concluded that India-Russia relations suffered from stagnation. A thought-provoking analysis by a Russian scholar (Fyodor Lukyanov) argued that India valued its independence and had the economic clout or capability to pursue an independent policy. Hence, India rates to be 'one of the new poles' in the world order. But he also took the view that India did not dare to pursue 'a really pro-active policy', with New Delhi taking 'evasive positions... hiding behind general statements.' He depicted India 'as a discerning bride desired by all' and concluded that 'Moscow still enjoys certain advantages, in the competition for India.'

Similarly, India's view of Russia's role is worth noticing. It is noteworthy that Indian analysts cannot help comparing today's Russia with the Soviet Union of the past. A general feeling amongst some of them is that Russia is essentially interested in Europe and in its immediate neighbourhood. Nevertheless, Russia is still viewed as a crucial player on the world stage, a fellow emerging economy, and a time-tested friend with which India should continue to strengthen and consolidate its relationship.

India-Russia relations have been free from bilateral disputes. They have been flourishing as 'a special and privileged strategic partnership.' Their tenor and trajectory are moulded not only by what the two countries do or do not do between themselves, but also by the pattern of relationships involving other major powers such as US, China, EU and Japan. Hence, a need to study and investigate the impact of this factor on India-Russia's mutual perceptions and cooperation is crucial.

In this context, two points may be made regarding the multilateral setting. Firstly, India's interest in securing the permanent membership of UN Security Council is supported by Russia, but an expectation is strongly been expressed by the Indian side that Russia needs to do more—and be seen to be doing more—in the desired direction. Secondly, concerning three other organizations i.e. RIC (Russia, India and China), BRICS (Brazil, Russia, India, China and South Africa) and EAS (East Asia Summit), Russia and India could consider stepping up their coordination and cooperation, a path that would promote mutual benefit on a large canvass.

On the bilateral plane, India and Russia need to examine how and in which specific areas the two countries should endeavour to do better. Defence, energy (including civilian nuclear energy), connectivity and economic relations seem to offer attractive possibilities. In these and other areas, bilateral cooperation should rise to meet its optimal potential. Besides, more cooperation in the area of public diplomacy, media links, tourism, and civil society connections could yield rich dividends, particularly because public awareness in India about Russia of today is highly limited. Above all, dialogue involving strategic communities of the two countries needs to be expanded.

**Rajiv K. Bhatia**

# Contents

## SECTION II
### Perceptions on Regional Issues

## Contributors

**Rajiv K. Bhatia**, Director General, Indian Council of World Affairs, New Delhi.

**Angira Sen Sarma** is Research Fellow, Indian Council of World Affairs, New Delhi.

**Baladas Ghoshal** holds the ICCR Chair in Indian Studies at the Russian State University for the Humanities, Moscow.

**Gulshan Sachdeva** is Professor of European Studies at the Centre for European Studies, School of International Studies, Jawaharlal Nehru University, New Delhi.

**Indrani Talukdar** is Research Fellow, Indian Council of World Affairs, New Delhi.

**Nandan Unnikrishnan** is Vice President in Observer Research Foundation, Centre for International Relations, New Delhi.

**Pankaj Jha** is Research Fellow, Indian Council of World Affairs, New Delhi.

**Shamma Jain** is Joint Secretary, Indian Council of World Affairs, New Delhi.

**Vinay Shukla** is an India-based Freelance Journalist and Eurasia Analyst.

**Vijay Sakhuja** is Director (Research), Indian Council of World Affairs, New Delhi.

# Introduction

The strategic partnership between India and Russia is 'a natural phenomenon' and its significance lies in mutual trust and commonality of views. Both partners have immense potential and can play a major role in the international arena.

India and Russia believe that the new world order is a multi-polar world and that no one country can lead the global system alone. However, they are cautious about the world order albeit the ongoing transitions and collaborate in global and bilateral issues.

This edited volume emerges from ICWA delegation's visit to Moscow where it held detailed discussions with Moscow State Institute of International Relations (MGIMO) and Russian International Affairs Council (RIAC) in May 2013, Russia. It focuses on the many facets of the bilateral relationship between India and Russia and their approach towards the international system. This compilation of papers highlights the high points as well as the low points of this strategic partnership.

The volume has been divided into two sections: Section I highlights the bilateral relationship between India and Russia and Section II emphasises their perceptions on regional issues. Both the sections are intertwined with each other.

There is a strong element of continuity in the bilateral relationship in the backdrop of an emerging multi-polar world, despite some lost opportunities due to some strains between India and Russia. New nuances have appeared between India and Russia over a period of time. The volume shows the importance of enhancing India and

Russia partnership by strengthening bilateral areas such as defence and exploring other areas for collaboration. The defence relationship between India and Russia is an important facet of the strategic partnership, which is further enhanced through the many defence agreements the two countries have agreed on. Hence, the reinforcement of their ties and new opportunities would help India and Russia to take their relationship to a qualitatively new level.

One thrust area of this volume is the futuristic trend-line that the authors attempt to portray to enhance India-Russia strategic partnership. It showcases the relevance of regions such as Afghanistan, Asia-Pacific, Central Asia and Pakistan and multilateral foras such as BRICS (Brazil, Russia, India, China and South Africa), SCO (Shanghai Cooperation Organisation), G-20 etc.

The Asia-Pacific region appears to be Russia's dilemma where it faces a number of challenges due to its self-perceived image of being a Eurasian power. The impact of this dilemma is reflected in its foreign policy approaches in this region. India has established its footprint in the Asia-Pacific region and India and Russia can explore their future role in this region.

The post-2014 Afghanistan presents a major challenge for India and Russia. After the US led International Security Assistance Force (ISAF) withdraws, India and Russia can play an important role in the reconstruction process of Afghanistan through their bilateral engagement. Likewise, Central Asia would play an important role post-2014 in this region. These countries have the capability to become the platform for India-Russia cooperation through joint initiatives in the region.

South Asia is witnessing a rekindled partnership between Russia and Pakistan. Pakistan's role would be important post-2014 for the stability and reconstruction of Afghanistan. The rationale behind Russia's engagement with Pakistan arises from at least two reasons i.e. drug trafficking and Islamic insurgency problems that have implications for Russia and its neighbourhood. For Pakistan, the rationale behind its engagement with Russia is to lessen its dependency on the US. The bilateral relationship between India and Russia is 'time-tested' and has withstood many challenges; however Russia's emerging relationship with Pakistan, would be a litmus test for the India-Russia strategic partnership.

**Vijay Sakhuja and Indrani Talukdar**

# Section I

## India-Russia: Bilateral Relationship

# 1
# India-Russia Relations

## Looking Ahead

*Nandan Unnikrishnan*

It is a cliché to say that India and Russia have a time-tested partnership, but a cliché worth repeating in the current context when the importance of this relationship is often unacknowledged in Indian strategic discussions.

This relationship has maintained a basic continuity despite the upheavals of the early 1990s, probably because of unprecedented uncertainty in international affairs. However, the level of trust has developed between the two countries in nearly 40 years of cooperation before the collapse of the Soviet Union. The development of this trust and understanding was probably also aided by India and Russia not sharing borders, not having territorial claims over each other and having never fought a war.

Moreover, developments in Russia's historical evolution have had a direct bearing on India's evolution. For instance, the revolution of 1917 gave a direct fillip to the Indian freedom struggle and the victory over Fascism, in which the Soviet Union played a critical part in what eventually led to the end of British colonialism in India.

During the Cold War, there were close diplomatic, military, economic and cultural ties between India and the USSR. The USSR played a key role in bolstering India's economic development and contributed to its security through supply of arms. The Soviet Union consistently supported India in all international fora on the Kashmir issue.

After the collapse of the Soviet Union, both India and Russia focussed on internal reforms. This led to an almost exclusive focus on the West by both countries. Coupled with the new Russian government's attempts to work out its place in the post-Cold War world, it now appears almost natural that there was a hiatus in Indo-Russian bilateral relations. However, this trend stalled by 1993 and a reversal began. With Vladimir Putin's ascendency to Presidency, this trend received a further boost.

To understand where the relationship stands today, it will be necessary to look at a number of issues that comprise the relationship.

## Political Relations

The first of issue is political cooperation. There are virtually no differences in the way New Delhi and Moscow view the world (except for a brief period when shortly after the break-up of the USSR, Russia tried to maintain an equidistance between India and Pakistan). The two countries share similar views on building a multi-polar world and changing the architecture of global governance to reflect the realities of today's world—the emergence of new powers and the relative decline of the West. President Putin stated that 'India is our candidate number one in terms of enlarging the geographical representation of the Security Council'.[1] Russia supports India's bid for a permanent seat on the UN Security Council as well as India's membership of the Nuclear Suppliers Group (NSG), the Shanghai Cooperation Organisation (SCO) and Asia Pacific Economic Community (APEC). The two countries also cooperate in various groupings like the G-20, BRICS, the SCO and Russia-India-China (RIC) trilateral.

There is a convergence of views on regional issues as well. For instance on Afghanistan, Russia and India have shared similar views. Likewise they share similar concerns about terrorism and instability in Central Asia. The only apparent difference of opinion in recent times has been on Syria.

## Military-Technical Cooperation

The second important strand of the relationship is military-technical cooperation. Indo-Russian defence cooperation goes back to 1962, when India purchased the MIG 21 aircraft. Subsequently, the two countries agreed on licensed production of MIGs in India. This developed into a relationship in which India sourced nearly 90 per cent of its military hardware from the Soviet Union. Till the collapse of the Soviet Union, the defence relationship was essentially a buyer-seller relationship—India bought equipment at reasonably cheap prices with low interest loans.

It would appear until then that India was really the sole beneficiary of this relationship. However, the true value of the military-technical relationship with India was realized by Russia after the break-up of the Soviet Union. Indian orders played a critical role in maintaining the Russian arms industry, which was on the verge of collapse.

With India being one of the top arms importers in the world in the last few years, the defence relationship is important for Russia and its arms industry. For India, what makes the relationship special is that Russia is willing to supply India with military platforms that no other country will consider providing, for example, the nuclear powered submarines. The Indian military may also use the Russian GLOSSNAS system. In addition, unlike some other suppliers, Russia has not supplied weapons to India's potential adversaries that could tilt the balance in their favour.

India is about 70 per cent dependent on Russian arms today.[2] But dependence on Russian arms is likely to fall to 60 per cent according to the Indian Ministry of External Affairs.[3] Over the last four decades, the value of India-Russia military technical cooperation has amounted to over US$ 35 billion.[4]

However, some questions have been raised about the future of bilateral military-technical cooperation. This is primarily because of India's strategic decision to diversify the sources of its defence procurements.

India is now in a position to buy more advanced weapons, but is also in the process of indigenising its arms industry. India's Defence

Procurement Policy (DPP), which requires foreign vendors to offset about 30 per cent of their orders, is another challenge in the way of strengthening the Indo-Russian defence relationship.

Other reasons for the decline in military-technical cooperation are the delays in deliveries, defective parts and renegotiation of prices by the Russians. There are several examples of this, including the delivery of T-90 tanks in 2005 without a firing missile system and with overheating problems. The delay and renegotiation of price of *Admiral Gorshkov/INS Vikramaditya* is another example. Russia's reluctance to participate in tenders and the cumbersome process of signing contracts for supply of arms have also contributed to this downturn. Russia's reluctance to participate in global arms tenders floated by India is yet another impediment.

Although these problems of delays and changes in pricing are not unique to Russian supplies, the sudden emergence of these in the public domain have negatively affected public perceptions about Russia-India relations in military-technical cooperation.

However, the picture is not all gloomy. There are several positive signs in the defence relationship. The first is that Russia and India are already collaborating on the Fifth Generation Aircraft. The BrahMos supersonic cruise missile system and these was developed under a joint patent, has already produced excellent weapons, which are being inducted into the Indian armed forces. These weapons can also be marketed worldwide. Fourteen countries already have reportedly evinced interest in acquiring the BrahMos missile.

Another joint venture is the development of a Multi-Role Transport Aircraft (MTA). There are plans to sell these aircrafts to third countries. Further, In August 2012, India and Russia signed a MoU for a Joint Venture to produce "SMERCH" rockets in India.[5]

The two countries also conducted joint exercises like the 4th 'INDRA' exercise by their armies in Buryatia, Russia, in August 2012, and the joint naval exercise 'INDRA' held off the Mumbai coast in December 2012.[6]

Sales to India account for 40 per cent of Russia's annual defence sales and this is likely to increase to over 50 per cent in the next few years given the current pipeline of contracts.[7] Moreover, Russia is likely to remain India's largest defence partner for at least the next few years as the two countries have already signed arms deals worth about US$ 11 billion and have established several important joint ventures.[8]

Another positive aspect is the increasing focus on the transfer of technology, modernization of existing equipment, and access to the latest equipment and weaponry in the Russian arsenal.[9]

In military-technical cooperation, the two governments have to manage expectations of the Russian military-industrial complex against what will be actually purchased and thereafter the portrayal of this in the public domain.

Since economic ties between Russia and India are not commensurate with the potential of their strategic partnership, sustaining military-technical cooperation acquires even greater importance.

Therefore, the causes of the decline in cooperation in this sector have to be addressed with great care by both India and Russia, as also understanding the constraints on both. Another limitation is the rapidly developing Russia-China military relationship, which will arouse distrust in India if technology commensurate with what is provided to India is supplied to China. Similarly, Russia's suspicions about Indo-US relations, particularly in the military sphere, could negatively affect the relationship.

## Cooperation in High Technology

New Delhi and Moscow have also been cooperating in various high technology areas. Under the Integrated Long Term Programme (ILTP), the largest scientific collaboration India has with any other country (signed in 1987). India and Russia cooperate in joint projects, hold joint workshops and seminars and exchange scientists. The programme has led to the "generation of new knowledge, development of products, facilities and designs through implementation of over 500 joint projccts and joint centres of excellence".[10]

Space has been a traditional area of cooperation. Russia and India had cooperated on Chandrayaan-I and are cooperating on Chandrayaan-II as well as India's Human Space Flight Program. NIS-GLONASS and Bharat Sanchar Nigam Ltd. and Mahanagar Telephone Nigam Ltd. have signed a MoU for a pilot project to assess the GLONASS using BSNL/MTNL ground infrastructure. If successful, this would pave the way for using GLONASS in sectors like disaster management, intelligent transportation, telephony and long-distance communications.[11] Other areas of cooperation are biotechnology and nanotechnology.

The India-Russia High Technology Forum has brought together high-tech projects from both countries. Russian scientific institutions have developed several technologies but do not have the skills to either market them or adapt them to civilian use. This is one area where India and Russia can work together.

## Economic Ties

Economic ties are the fourth strand in the Indo-Russian strategic partnership. Economic ties were the cornerstone of India's relations with the Soviet Union and trade touched US$ 5.5 billion in 1985. It is barely double that at about US$ 11 billion according to Russian statistics. Compared to this, Indo-US trade in 1990 was US$ 5.6 billion and now stands at almost US$ 100 billion (including trade in services). While India's trade with China was US$ 0.2 billion in 1990, today it is around US$ 80 billion. While trade with the EU stood at 26.96 billion Euros in 2002, today it is around 76 billion Euros. Mutual investments also fall much below the potential. Russian investment in India amounts to around US$ 4 billion (mostly in the telecommunications and infrastructure sectors), while Indian investment in Russia amounts to around US$ 6.5 billion, almost of it is in the energy sector.[12]

In a globalised economy, economic ties form the basis of any sustained strategic partnership. To strengthen and deepen the strategic partnership, India and Russia have to understand the constraints within which economic ties have to develop.

The first of these constraints is the transport bottleneck. India's troubled relationship with Pakistan and the continued instability in Afghanistan have contributed to the access problem. Though the North-South corridor is an option, this will take time to fructify. Given this situation, India and Russia should focus on items, which do not require surface transport and till the transport bottlenecks are overcome, concentrate on investments, particularly through joint ventures.

There are nascent signs of this, but there needs to be a greater push by India to invest in agriculture, IT, Pharmaceuticals, etc. in Russia. Russia, on the other hand, needs to invest more in energy, metallurgy and infrastructure projects in India.

Infrastructure development is a huge opportunity as India is poised to spend over US$1 trillion on infrastructure over the next five years. Some Russian companies like Transstroy (which has invested about US$ 3 billion) are already involved in infrastructure projects in India. However, there is potential for more investments.

Another problem is that business elites from both countries find the processes not adequately transparent and requiring heavy investment in political liaison. Serious government efforts are required to ease entry barriers into markets, particularly investments.

Efforts have to be made to explain to businessmen on both sides about bilateral economic realities. Niggling problems like visa restrictions also have to be addressed. The economic relationship is dominated by state-to-state trade or PSU-to-PSU trade. In order for economic ties to truly take off, the private sector (which accounts for 70 per cent of the economy in India)[13] needs to get more involved and it is important that the governments encourage and facilitate the relationship.

## Energy Cooperation

Energy cooperation would appear to be a natural area of cooperation between Russia and India due to the complementarity between Russia's huge reserves and India's need for energy. India's ONGC

Videsh Limited is a stakeholder in the Sakhalin-1 project and is seeking a stake in the Sakhalin-3 project through a joint venture with Rosneft. ONGC Videsh Limited also acquired Imperial Energy in 2009, though it is now facing problems and has so far been a loss-making venture for ONGC.

However, the realities of geography have come in the way of greater cooperation in this area. This is also the area where India's troubled relationship with Pakistan and instability in the region is felt most acutely. However, this could be addressed if India and Russia were given greater access to each other's energy sectors, upstream and downstream.

For instance, India could enter into the production of Russian oil and gas and use what is produced to enter into swap deals with other producers or consumers. India could also help build petrochemical projects in Russia instead of just exporting raw crude and gas. This would allow Russia to export value-added goods like plastics. India has the skills and has one of the most advanced petrochemical industries in the world—the Jamnagar oil refinery in Gujarat is the single largest grassroots refinery in the world. Russia, on the other hand, could help in hydrocarbon exploration in India and in building pipelines across India.

Nuclear energy cooperation is a strategic aspect of the Indo-Russian partnership. India and the Soviet Union signed a nuclear cooperation deal in 1988 This was updated later and extended with other agreements, such as the 2002 agreement for the construction of two nuclear reactors by Russia at Kudankulam.[14] According to press reports four more nuclear reactors are being planned.

In 2009, Moscow and New Delhi reached a long-term agreement for expanding civil nuclear cooperation that is free from any restrictions on India and guarantees it against any curbs in the future.[15] As per this agreement, Russia would "ensure transfer of technology and uninterrupted uranium fuel supplies to [India]'s nuclear reactors".[16] Consequently, Russia made its first uranium delivery to India in April 2009. In 2010, India and Russia reached an agreement to build 16 nuclear power plants in India in the next 15 years.[17]

At the global level, Russia has never imposed sanctions on India for its nuclear programme and has stood by it at critical times. Russia has also been supportive of India's entry into the Nuclear Suppliers Group. India is acutely aware of this even while seeking to display fairness in its dealings with the world in awarding contracts for nuclear power stations.

However, of late, India's Nuclear Liability Law appears to have stymied cooperation in this sector. Russia must understand that India cannot appear to favour Russia over Indian domestic laws, particularly the Nuclear Liability Law. Another hurdle that Russia faces is the competition from other countries with which India has signed civil nuclear deals such as France and the US.[18]

## Cultural Relations

Cultural and people-to-people relations were strong during Soviet times. The Indo-Soviet association used to be very active; publications like "The Soviet Land" and "Sputnik" were widely available. There used to be large and regular academic exchanges and tens of thousands of Indian students studied in Russian universities. Hundreds of Russian experts and specialists lived in India and helped build dams, coal mines, industries, etc. Russian language courses used to have the largest number of applicants. Therefore, the Russian speaking diaspora was large in India.

However, the picture does not look so good today. Enrolment for Russian language courses is low. The two countries have lost salience in the imagination of the elites in both countries as they are, for differing reasons, focussed on the West. Therefore, there are serious information gaps about each other. Part of the problem here is the matter of perception which both governments should address.

There is a need for exchange of information about each other in the mass media and greater coverage of each other must be encouraged. Academic interactions must be enhanced. India and Russia should create an Eminent Persons Group that could advise the government on addressing some of these problems.

The governments should encourage the creation of easy and cheap tourism to both countries in order to re-acquaint the people with the rich cultural heritage of both countries. This would help in broad-basing the relationship and in increasing the number of stakeholders interested in stronger ties between the two countries.

## Conclusion

In conclusion, it is important to quote India's former National Security Adviser and Foreign Secretary J.N. Dixit, who wrote the following:

> "Leaving aside the convergence of interests and attitudes ... the fundamental reality is that though Russia may have lost its position as a super power in Cold War equations, it is still a big power in terms of the ingredients of such power. It is territorially large, it strategically abuts on Central Asia, China and Iran, an area of political, security and economic interests to India. Russia is endowed with enormous natural resources, technological capacities, trade potential and over and above all a highly talented reservoir of human resources. It still is the most important military power in the world after the United States. ... It is logical, therefore, for India to cultivate and nurture relationship with Russia in the context of historical experience, current policy orientations and tangible mutuality of interests and mutual benefits. Realism requires that Russia remains a country of priority in India's external relations".

It is clear from the above that Russia is of critical significance to India. However, if this relationship is to overcome the current drift and blossom, then it is equally important that Russia recognises the importance of India. A mutual understanding of each other's worth will be the appropriate to take the relationship to a qualitatively new level.

## NOTES

1. Quoted in Richard Weitz. "The Maturing of Russia-India Defence Relations", *Journal of Defence Studies*, Vol. 6, no. 3 (2012), p. 78.
2. Katherine Foshko Tsan. "Re-Energizing the Indian-Russian Relationship: Opportunities and Challenges for the 21st Century", *Jindal Journal of International Affairs*, Vol. 2, no. 1 (August 2012), p. 144.
3. Katherine Foshko Tsan. *ibid.*, p. 150.
4. Weitz. "The Maturing of Russia-India" p. 79, *op. cit.*
5. Interview with Indian Ambassador to Russia, Ajai Malhotra, January 15, 2013. Available at http://indrus.in/articles/2013/01/15/indo-ussian_ties_based_on_substance_not_rhetoric_ajai_malhotra_21633.html.
6. *Ibid.*
7. Foshko Tsan. "Re-Energizing the Indian-Russian Relationship", p. 150, *op. cit.*
8. Weitz. "The Maturing of Russia-India", p. 90, *op. cit.*
9. Foshko Tsan, p. 148, *op. cit.*
10. "Indo-Russian S&T Cooperation". http://indianembassy.ru/index.php/science-technology/indo-russian-s-t-cooperation.
11. Interview with Indian Ambassdor to Russia, *op. cit.*
12. http://indianembassy.ru/index.php?option=com_content&view=article&id=705&Itemid=705&lang=en
13. Foshko Tsan. "Re-Energizing the Indian-Russian Relationship", p. 144, *op. cit.*
14. *Ibid*, p. 157.
15. *Ibid*, p. 158.
16. *Ibid*, Quoted in Katherine Foshko Tsan, 'Re-Energizing the Indian-Russian Relationship: Opportunities and Challenges for the 21st Century', *Jindal Journal of International Affairs*, Volume 2, Issue 1, August 2012, p. 158.
17. *Ibid*, p. 158.
18. *Ibid*, p. 159.

# 2
# New Contours of India-Russia Special and Privileged Strategic Partnership

*Vinay Shukla*

India and Russia have a long and eventful history of bilateral relations, never marred by conflict of national interests. Late Soviet leader Leonid Brezhnev during his last visit to India in 1981 at a public rally had said in New Delhi that the friendship between the two countries is not the friendship of the two governments, rather is the friendship between the peoples of the two countries. Perhaps, this sentiment was the key driving force, which revived and elevated the bilateral relations to the current level of 'privileged strategic partnership'. After hiatus of early 1990s, the bilateral relations again began to gather steam.

Moving away from the moment of Soviet collapse, many new nuances have appeared in the bilateral relationship, mainly due to the diverse foreign policy vectors of post-Soviet Russian Federation and contemporary India in the wake of the geopolitical vacuum caused by the fragmentation of the world's second super power and the collapse of bipolar global security architecture. Here, it would be fair to note that the shift in Kremlin's policy began back in the times of USSR, when after the death of Soviet leader Leonid Brezhnev in November 1982, the customary slogan hailing Indo-Soviet friendship was already missing among the 1983 May Day slogans of the Central Committee of Communist Party of Soviet Union (CC CPSU) under new General Secretary, Yuri Andropov.

Russia traditionally has had many historical problems in relations with its immediate neighbours in Europe and the West in general. However, after joining G-8, it had reoriented its foreign policy towards former Cold War rivals in order to rediscover its European identity and seeking Western technology for the modernisation of highly militarised and ineffective economy inherited from the USSR. The Cryogenic Deal with India was the first victim of Russia's westward course, when in spite of President Boris Yeltsin's assurances in New Delhi in January 1993, few months later under the US pressure, Moscow, citing the Missile Technology Control Regime (MTCR) obligations, refused to transfer cryogenic technology for the development of indigenous booster stage of the geostationary satellite launch vehicles (SLV) by ISRO.

Many Indian apprehensions about the reliability of the post-Soviet Russia as a long-term partner especially as supplier of defence hardware were not misplaced. If erratic supplies of spares for the Soviet-origin hardware partly had objective reasons as many OEM units were left behind in other Soviet republics, the 'Gorshkov'—'Vikramaditya' saga has done a huge damage to Moscow's prestige in India.

In spite of 'wrinkles in the moods' caused by concrete cases like delay in delivery of retrofitted 'Gorshkov', ongoing reformatting of Russia and India's roles in the shaping global political, security and economic architecture, the two nations are virtually interacting in all the spheres of human activity. Their interaction at international and multilateral fora like UN, BRICS and RIC is of great importance for ensuring global peace, security and stable economic development.

In the present scenario, the UN remains the only multilateral democratic body in the world, although its effectiveness is marred by the fact that its apex body—Security Council, remains ossified in its post-World War-II apotheosis and does not reflect the contemporary realities. Russia was among the first P-5 nations to name India as a deserving candidate for a permanent seat in the expanded Security Council. However, Moscow is not very keen to rush in the process of reforming it, since it challenge its ability in retaining the decisive say on key global issues through the veto power. Moscow also fears alienation in the expanded Security Council, which would have on board at least two more US allies in case of its reform.

The reality is that India along with other members of G-4, i.e. Brazil, Germany and Japan is keen for the earliest expansion of the UNSC, while Russia would actually prefer a *status quo* as long as the 'widest consensus' is evolved – almost an impossible goal – given the regional rivalries like India-Pakistan, Germany-Italy and Japan-China.

Unfortunately, the trilateral—Russia-India-China mechanism, which could have become an influential tool in ensuring regional and global security and stability, is losing its relevance as India is the only non-UNSC member in it. This creates the impression of India being given the role of a junior partner in Moscow's interaction with the two Asian giants.

It is natural that dynamics of their growing role in the ever changing world and instability in the proximity of their physical borders and geopolitical frontiers could lead to differences and even friction in bilateral relations due to clash of interests over some local political and economic issues. However, the relations are mature enough to resolve any such issues amicably.

At times Russia is overreacting (at least the experts' opinion vented in Russian publications indicate this) to India-US bonhomie. Shortly after the Soviet collapse, even before that under President Mikhail Gorbachev's *New thinking* and *Perestroika*, Moscow's engagement with the US and Europe for improving bilateral relations in the post-Cold war era had virtually devalued the special relationship with New Delhi. However, New Delhi's attempts to seek a rapport and improve relations with Washington were seen in Moscow as 'India going into America's lap', defence tenders lost by Russia, were used to substantiate this argument by the Russian experts community.

Moscow needs to reconcile with reality that like Russia, which identifies itself as part of the European civilisation, India *de facto* is a part of the Anglo-Saxon world specially this positioning became more prominent in the backdrop of growing clout of the so called great Indian middle class. After all there are about 8 million Indians or peoples of Indian origin settled in the US and given the tradition of their extended families and relatives, the number of Indians having family and emotional linkages with the US and business and economic interests in that country could even match the entire population of Russia. It would be natural for the Government of India to adopt a proactive policy vis-à-vis the US and be in a position to safeguard the interests of its nationals.

Similarly, India should be ready to at least understand Russia's aspirations to have close ties with its giant Asian neighbour China and normalise relations with Pakistan within the bilateral and multilateral framework of Organisation of Islamic Countries (OIC) and Shanghai Cooperation Organisation (SCO). However, New Delhi should also be convinced that its sensitivities will not be overlooked or compromised for the narrow vested interests of a section of Russian military industrial complex (MIC).

## Defence Cooperation

Indo-Russian defence cooperation is based on long-term Inter-Governmental Military-Technical Cooperation (MTC) Programme and remains a solid pillar of the bilateral strategic partnership. In spite of delays and cost-escalation in upgradation of Admiral Gorshkov aircraft carrier, Russia in foreseeable future will remain not only a major source of defence hardware, but also highly sensitive cutting-edge military technologies, usually denied by other foreign vendors.

The development of state-of-the-art Sukhoi Su-30MKI (I-stands for India) multirole fighter has opened a new chapter in India- Russia defence cooperation in mid-1990s. This project marked the beginning of transformation of 'buyer-seller' relationship into dynamic joint research, development, production and marketing. Su-30MKI and its modifications are Russian defence industry's latest and popular export item to third countries and many aircraft (with the exception of China) are equipped with avionics and sensors supplied by Hindustan Aeronautics Limited (HAL).

While working on the Su-30MKI project, the Indian and Russian engineers and experts accumulated a rich experience in bilateral cooperation, which allowed them to move ahead with the sophisticated Multirole Transport Aircraft (MTA) project providing for the joint R&D, manufacture and marketing of state-of-the-art aircraft capable of taking off and landing in any conditions including high altitude airstrips in Himalayas. The joint cooperation on the fifth generation fighter aircraft (FGFA) project based on Sukhoi's T-50 PAKFA prototype is another milestone in transformation of relations in MTC.

One of the specialities of defence cooperation with Moscow is that it offers India its military hardware which is yet to find way into its own armed forces. Russia has built six Talwar class stealth frigates. To cut costs on the new project, Russia has also decided to build six stealth frigates of this project for its Black Sea Fleet. The successful integration of the highly effective Indian equipment into the Talwar Class frigates has prompted Moscow to buy it for its own frigates too. According to diplomatic sources, Bharat Electronics Limited (BEL) is expected to supply US$ 30-40 million worth of equipment per vessel to the Russian frigates.

During his visit to Moscow in 2003, Prime Minister Atal Bihari Vajpayee had told the local Indian community that Russia and India have agreed to jointly work on highly advanced futuristic weapons and defence technologies. A good example is the BrahMos supersonic cruise missiles which is expected to remain unmatched in foreseeable future. Russia has also agreed to give India access to military segment of its space based GLONASS navigation system which provides the opportunity for precision guidance for ballistic missiles during flight. Besides, India and Russia are jointly working on satellite killer microwave weapons and 'green lasers' for encrypted communications with submarines. Russia's cooperation in building indigenous nuclear powered submarine 'Arihant' is also in public domain.

With India seeking self-reliance in defence, the time for big-ticket defence deals could eventually end. But the Indo-Russian MTC is likely to continue to remain the pivot of strategic partnership if the two nations continue to advance along the established trends and adopt new approaches for mutual benefit. India also needs to pay attention to Russian armed forces modernisation programme till 2020 and beyond. A mutually beneficial cooperation in this could also benefit the two countries.

## Trade and Economic Cooperation: Two Decades of Lost Opportunities

The bilateral trade and economic cooperation is a weak leg of the privileged strategic partnership. At the highest political level there is an acute realisation of this fact and several attempts have been made in the past to rectify the situation, which includes expanding the trade basket and forays into hi-tech innovative sectors. The leadership of the two countries had set the goal of boosting the bilateral trade of US$ 10 billion by 2010 and this target was missed. In 2012, the Russian statistics service registered US$ 11 billion trade, and the two countries have vowed to achieve US$ 20 billion trade turnover by 2015. It is difficult to say at this juncture, how realistic is the goal.

In the above context, it is useful to recall that Indian exports to the USSR were above US$ 5 billion in 1990. India was Soviet Union's biggest trade partner in the third world, while Federal Republic of Germany topped in the developed world, and still remains there.

Today three decades later, its bilateral trade with Russia stands at less than US$ 10 billion. According to data posted on the MEA website, in 2011, Russian exports to India amounted to US$ 6.1 billion and imports from India to Russia amounted to US$ 2.8 billion. During January-October 2012, the bilateral trade amounted to US$ 8.72 billion. The two-way cumulative investment between India and Russia stands at approximately US$ 7.8 billion.

## Searching for Complementarities

Historically, the two countries were never trade partners in its true meaning. The Soviet era trade with shiploads of third class shoes with cardboard soles and jute bags, tea and coffee, and cotton garments was essentially a barter trade through a clearing house mechanism of debt repayment rupee account.

In the hay days, Russian shops were full of a vast range of quality Indian consumer products and pharmaceuticals, the driving force was Iraqi crude. Iraq used to pay for Soviet arms and military hardware through its crude oil, most of which was shipped directly to India for its energy needs. The payment was again made in Indian rupees, which were spent by USSR for purchasing Indian goods for own market or sourcing supplies for its allies, notably in rebuilding post-war Vietnam.

The whole scheme busted in August 1990 after Iraq's occupation of Kuwait, followed by the UN authorised US-led operation the *Desert Storm* in January 1991 and sanctions on Iraq. Stuck in the middle of *Perestroika* the Soviet government had no money to pay for imports from India.

### India's Exchange Challenges

As a result of various restrictions in imports from India, the Russian Finance Ministry decided to disburse US dollar denominated rupee funds at a discount, at a much lower rate than the official rate of exchange. Although, some Indian companies in Russia did utilise this opportunity, but most of the funds were picked up by multinationals. Instead of promoting exports to Russia to retain the market share of still highly valued Indian goods and commodities by the local consumer and processing industry, India added additional restrictions, obviously in good faith to protect drainage of foreign exchange. However, in the longer perspective it simply led to the loss of Russian market, even in the tea sector where Sri Lanka has long overtaken India.

### The Way Ahead

Over the last two decades, with the efforts of the two governments, most of the bottlenecks—like banking, insurance and investment protection—in bilateral India-Russia trade have been removed.

However, the problems of poor logistics, proper transport infrastructure still remain to be resolved due to delays (partly due to US and EU sanctions on Iran) in operationalising the International North-South Transport Corridor (INSTC) for seamless connectivity. Albeit, the existing air routes provide a viable mode of exporting high value and value-added items like fresh cut flowers and pharmaceuticals to Russia.

Since post-Soviet, Russia lacks round-the-year port facilities in its European parts, its Pacific ports like Vladivostok and Nakhodka can be used for trade with its far eastern and eastern parts right up to the Urals.

At the same time India and Russia would have to evolve a new strategy to revive and develop their economic cooperation and trade to tap their potential of complementarities for sustained development of the two nations. Perhaps this task should not be left only for the private business.

This strategic approach would require capacity building by India and Russia on each-other's territory, besides simple investments in their economies. For example, like in the case of energy cooperation by way of investments in Russia's hydrocarbons assets, India needs to invest in Russia's raw materials resources production and processing, agriculture and mining, so that finished or semi-finished products could be imported for the needs of the national economy.

President Vladimir Putin has set the goal of doubling Russia's GDP by 2020 and complete the modernisation of the post-Communist nation's economy and defence. This plan opens great opportunities for interaction in almost all the spheres of human activity, but India's capacity to cash on them remains questionable. The main challenge lies in how successfully India would be able to compete with China and other rivals including the West and East Asian countries for the immense energy resources and mineral wealth of Urals and Siberia.

Similarly, if Russia is to retain and enhance its presence in India, it should join long-term investment projects like the Delhi-Mumbai Industrial Corridor (DMIC) project and set up its own exclusive economic zone for the Russian industry taking interest not only in the Indian market, but also catering to the needs of domestic consumers.

Russia has one of the highest per capita intellectual potential in the world and is a technology powerhouse. Hundreds, if not thousands of little known innovators are busy in developing cutting edge technologies of the future in many incubators and special economic zones set up in Russia's remote corners, away from Moscow's glitterati. The Indian small and medium scale industries must be helped in looking for partners among them to produce and market hi-tech products.

The idea of a Free Trade Agreement (FTA) with Belarus-Russia-Kazakhstan Customs Union, recently being paddled by New Delhi, could take decades in its materialisation, as the aforesaid logistics and transport bottlenecks could become the main stumbling block. Secondly, the FTA would be viable only if the volume of trade is at a sustainable level.

### Creating Economic Avenues

In spite of regular contacts between the commerce and industries bodies of the two countries like Federation of Indian Chambers of Commerce and Industry (FICCI), Confederation of Indian Industries (CII), Russian Chamber of Commerce and Industry (RCCI) and Russian Union of Industrialists and Entrepreneurs (RUIE), there are two basic mindsets among the business communities. A section of Indian business still think Russia is a third rate country not worth looking at, while others see some opportunities for trade, but complain about the high rate of crime, corruption and mafia. Russian business has a similar view of India. Not much has materialized from the creation of the joint CEOs Council as the negative stereotypes still prevail in the minds of potential businessmen.

It is an established fact that Russia—occupying almost one-sixth of the landmass on the planet, has world's richest mineral wealth deposits in its sparsely populated eastern parts. The Arctic region, which so far has been mainly dominated by Russia, with the advent of the global warming, has become the focus of attention and witnessing growing rivalry between global powers. India needs to have a stake in this hydrocarbons-rich region and Russia's Polar Urals mega-mining project for the extraction of untapped mineral deposits of the region for its long-term sustained development.

Trade and economic cooperation between India and Russia is of vital importance for meeting India's growth targets by 2025 to become a global economic giant by 2050 or it will have to buy the necessary Russian resources at prohibitive prices from the Chinese and Western corporations.

## Cultural and P2P Cooperation

Cultural and people-to-people (P2P) linkages have always been a key component of the traditional India-Russia ties; it would not be an exaggeration, that they are the impetus to the friendly and privileged strategic partnership, invisible but indispensable.

Perhaps these linkages at the human dimension were the main force, which kept the light of the friendship burning even when the Soviet Union collapsed and a new political and economic system emerged in the Russian Federation in the last decade of the 20th century. Simultaneously, India also underwent drastic changes albeit not as dramatic as in Russia. But the goodwill and friendship among the people helped weather those stormy times. Credit for this goes to previous generations of the statesmen, political, social and cultural activists, who created the groundwork.

However, the question today is whether the current generation would be leaving the same legacy for the future generations, who would be witnessing even more dramatic times, when the contemporary world order undergoes major transformations to accommodate new global powers and players in the multipolar world. Older and middle generations still remember the good old days of Hindi-Roosi Bhai-Bhai, but the younger generations are rapidly growing to replace them. In olden times, the governments of India and Soviet Union heavily invested to create an infrastructure to promote cultural and person-to-person cooperation among the people. In 1967, Institute of Russian Studies in the Jawaharlal Nehru University was created with the financial and technical assistance of the Soviet Government. Lot of emphasis was given to Russian Language and the best faculties from Russia were hired for the task of teaching the Indian students.

The Government of India has backed the creation of several boarding schools in Moscow and elsewhere in ex-USSR with focus on teaching Hindi and other Indian languages. Similarly, assistance in the form of visiting professors and books were provided to the then Institute of Oriental Languages, now Asia and Africa Institute of Moscow State University. The Jawaharlal Nehru Cultural Centre (JNCC) in Moscow was established with the efforts of Ambassador Triloki Nath Kaul and like the Russian Science and Culture centres in India, JNCC is deeply and devotedly involved in the promotion of the bilateral friendship through culture.

However, these efforts are not enough and require greater involvement of younger generations through mutual education programmes and exchanges. One of the reasons for Russia fast reclaiming its previous prestige as a global power is that thousands of foreign alumni of Russian universities and institutes are holding influential posts in their respective countries. In India, many top experts and officials in metallurgy, power engineering and of course, oil and gas sector have a record of studying in Russia. Although de-ideologised Russia has almost curtailed programmes for training foreign specialists, but it could look at it as an investment in future.

India, with its vast human resource could provide highly skilled force for the development and modernisation of the Russian economy. The ongoing shifts in Russia's ossified migration policy to absorb expatriate graduates of Russian higher educational and vocational institutions open new avenues for cultural and humanitarian interaction between the nations. Democratisation of the Russian migration regime and Indian policy of granting citizenship rights to overseas and Person of Indian Origin (PIO) card for the family members of the persons born in India have brought revolutionary changes in the lives of hundreds of mix families. Earlier, for every visit to each other country they required proper invitation and visa.

Russia needs to widely publicise the welcome changes in its migration policy.

Today the electronic and print media does not play a substantial role in bilateral cultural and humanitarian cooperation. Further, the bilateral stories are overloaded with negative overtones, to some extent they could be justified due to scarcity of positive dynamics in bilateral relations.

Although, leading Russian news agencies like ITAR-TASS and RIA Novosti maintain their bureaus in New Delhi, the footprint of their India coverage has drastically shrunk due to radical cuts in financing or probably loss of interest in the country. Plans of opening of Russian TV's bureau has been on for about a decade; the English language Russia Today (RT) channel has a bureau in New Delhi, but its broadcasts beamed to India are rather strange and give very little knowledge of Russia. Similarly, in 1990s there were nine Indian correspondents in Moscow representing a wide spectrum of Indian print media; but today, there are only two stringers. This shows a weakening of interest in Russia's part to understand India better at close quarters.

# 3
# Post-2014 Afghanistan

## Possible Areas of India-Russia Cooperation

*Gulshan Sachdeva*

It is expected that very soon a relatively new phase of Afghanistan project will begin. In the recent past, the country has witnessed diverse projects of nation building and socio-political transformation. The Soviet project of building communism in Afghanistan resulted in over a million dead and five million Afghan refugees, mainly in the neighbourhood. Similarly, when Pakistan pushed conservative Taliban regime in Afghanistan, the world faced disastrous consequences, including the 9/11 terrorist attacks in the United States. The current international project of building democracy and market economy is mandated by the United Nations and being implemented mainly by the western alliance led by the United States. So far, this endeavour has produced mixed results. Apart from installing a democratic government, the country has made significant achievements in infrastructure, education, women empowerment and the economy. However, the Taliban insurgency is gaining strength in many parts of the country and security situation has deteriorated. Despite a mixed picture, the future of Afghanistan looks more uncertain today than any time in the last one decade. One important reason for this uncertainty is that almost everyone involved in the Afghanistan project believes that by 2014 a significant number of coalition forces would have left the country, even if some American forces continue to stay in a few negotiated bases for longer periods mainly in non-combat missions. In June 2011, President Obama announced that the US policies had already accomplished most major goals and that drawdown of the US troops will begin in 2012. Despite doubts about the durability, the transition to Afghan leadership began, as planned, in July 2011, and is continuing. The security responsibility for many provinces and cities has already been handed over to Afghan authorities. According to a Pentagon report released in September 2012, about 76 per cent of Afghans were living in areas where the Afghan National Security Forces (ANSF) had begun to assume the lead for security.[1] This transition will be over by the end of 2014 and a new phase of Afghanistan project will begin. Because of unpredictable nature of these changes, analysts have built many future scenarios for Afghanistan. These include collapse of the present regime and Taliban takeover; partition of Afghanistan; continuation of present stalemate, power sharing with some elements of present insurgency, and an optimistic scenario of a smooth transition followed by a decade of transformation. In these circumstances, most recent discussions and writings on Afghanistan indicate that in the post-2014 phase, the country is going to face three major challenges—security, political and economic. In all three areas, enhanced Indian and Russian cooperation in Afghanistan could help the country meet these difficult challenges during its decade of transformation.

## India's Role in Reconstruction

With broad understanding that peaceful and stable Afghanistan is crucial for regional stability, India has been playing an active role in the reconstruction since 2002. So far it has pledged assistance worth about US$ 2 billion, with projects covering the whole of country mainly in the areas of road construction, power transmission lines, hydro electricity, agriculture, telecommunication, education, health and capacity building. Details of these projects can be classified under four major heads:

### *Infrastructure Projects*

One of the major infrastructural projects completed by India is construction of 218 km Zaranj-Delaram road project in the southwestern Afghanistan. This road has a strategic significance for India as it is going to facilitate movement of goods and services from Afghanistan to the Iranian border and, onward, to the Chahbahar Port. This road, together with 60 km of inner-city roads in Zaranj and Gurguri, was completed in January 2009 at a cost of US$ 150 million. During construction 6 Indians and 179 Afghans lost their lives due to insurgent attacks. Another major project, which was completed in 2009 was construction of 220 kV DC transmission line from Pul-e-Khumri to Kabul and a 220/110/20 kV sub-station at Chimtala. Built at the cost of US$120 million, this line has facilitated almost 24 hour power supply from the northern grid to Kabul city. Further, Indian engineers are also setting up additional 220/20 kV sub-stations at Charikar and Doshi along the Pule-e-khumri Kabul transmission line. With the Indian help, construction and commissioning of US$ 184 million, 42 MW Salma Dam power project on Hari Rud river in Herat province is also being constructed. The completion of this project is behind schedule. At the cost of US$ 180 million, Indian government is also going to construct Afghan Parliament building. It is expected that the building will be completed soon. It has also restored telecommunication infrastructure in 11 provinces and expanded national TV network by providing an uplink from Kabul and downlinks in all 34 provincial capitals. Earlier, it also supplied vehicles (400 buses and 200 mini-buses for mass urban transportation, 105 utility vehicles for municipalities) and 3 airbus aircrafts and spares to Ariana Afghan Airlines. The Indian government also supplied equipment for three sub-stations in Faryab province and for 125 km transmission line from Andhkhoi to Maimana plus rehabilitated Amir Ghazi and Quargah Reservoir Dam. It further helped in restoration/revamping of information set up, including setting up of Azadi (Freedom) printing press. Other infrastructure projects include solar electrification of 100 villages; construction of 5,000 MT cold storage in Kandahar; establishment of modern TV studio and 1,000 W TV transmitter in Jalalabad; setting up of a mobile TV satellite uplink and five TV relay centres in Nangarhar; digging 26 tube wells in 6 north-west provinces; drilling of 24 deep wells in Herat; planned construction of Radio television Afghanistan (RTA) building in Jalalabad and leasing of slot on Indian satellite INSAT3A for RTA telecast since 2004.

### *Humanitarian Assistance*

The Indian government is providing a daily supply of 100 g of fortified, high-protein biscuits to nearly 1.2 million children under a School Feeding Program. This programme is administered through the World Food Programme with the cost of US$ 460 million till 2012. It has also reconstructed Indira Gandhi Institute of Child Health in Kabul and is providing free medical consultation and medicines through 5 Indian Medical Missions in Kabul, Kandahar, Jalalabad, Heart and Mazar-e-Shrif to over 300,000 patients annually. Apart from supplying blankets, tents, medicines, vegetable seeds, etc. during 2002-2004, the Indian government also announced gift of 250,000 metric tonnes of wheat in 2009.

### *Education and Capacity Development*

India is playing an important role in this field through provision of 675 long-term university scholarships annually. These fellowships are sponsored by the Indian Council for Cultural Relations for under-graduate and postgraduate studies in India. In addition, 675 annual slots for short-term technical training courses are provided every year since 2006. At the January 2010 London Conference, Indian External Affairs Minister announced further 200 graduate and 100 post graduate/Ph.D. fellowships for 5 years in the field of agriculture and related fields. In 2005, the Habibia school in Kabul was reconstructed by India and about 9000 educational kits to students of this school were provided. Further, it provided 20,000 school desks to the Ministry of Education and laboratory equipments and sports goods to schools in Nimroz as well as teacher training and books to Kandahar and Khost Universities. In cooperation with the UNDP, the Indian government is also deputing 30 Indian civil servants as coaches and mentors annually under the Capacity for Afghan Public

Administration programme since 2007. It has also provided services of Indian banking experts to Da Afghan Bank and Millie Bank; Indian English teachers in 5 cities; vocational training to 1,000 Afghans (through the Confederation of Indian Industries); Women's Vocational Training Centre in Baghe-Zanana for training of 1,000 Afghan women; computer training centres, and established Hindi and English departments at Nangarhar university. Special training courses have also been provided to Afghan diplomats, dozens of civilian officials, police officers, teachers, and doctors and paramedics. In addition, Indian institutions are also providing training to Afghans in various fields through training programmes organised by many international agencies independently.

With the help of the Indian government, nearly 100 small development projects in the areas of agriculture, public health, rural development and education have also been implemented in 19 provinces of Afghanistan since 2006. In the first phase from 2006, 50 projects were implemented worth US$ 11,216,179; and in the second phase June 2008, 51 projects worth US$ 8,579,537 were initiated. In the new third phase in November 2012, Indian government announced new projects worth US$100 million for implementation. In 2002, India also contributed US$10 million to Afghan government budget and has also been contributing to the Afghan Reconstruction Trust Fund regularly since 2002. In 2005-06, it also provided 150 trucks, 15 ambulances, 120 jeeps, bullet proof jackets, bullet proof helmets, laser aim points, mine detectors, winter clothing, medicines, etc. to Afghan National Army. It also helped setting up of Common Facilities Service Centre and Tool Room at Pule-e-Charkhi Industrial Park and trained 5,000 self help groups in Balakh.

## Strategic Partnership

Enlarged Indian engagement in Afghanistan can easily be built on the "Strategic Partnership" agreement already signed by both in October 2011.[2] This was the first ever strategic partnership agreement signed by Afghanistan with any foreign country. Apart from capacity building support to the various departments in the three branches of government, including the Executive, Judiciary and the Parliament, the agreement points towards two major things. First, India has agreed 'as mutually determined' to assist in the training, equipping and capacity building programmes for Afghan national security forces. Secondly, it recognised that regional economic cooperation is vital for long-term economic prosperity of Afghanistan and the region. In addition, the agreement creates bilateral institutional mechanism consisting of annual summit meeting, regular political consultations led by foreign ministries of both countries and establishment of strategic dialogue on national security led by national security advisors of both countries. Although many of these things were already happening, still the agreement provided a concrete institutional mechanism and clear support for Afghan institutions for the years and decades to come.

## International Commitments and Role for India and Russia

At the Bonn and Istanbul conferences in 2011, both the international community as well as regional players re-affirmed their long-term commitment to the future of Afghanistan, which goes much beyond 2014. The Bonn Conference of December 2011 was attended by 85 countries and 15 international organisations. At the conference, all participants dedicated themselves to "deepening and broadening their historic partnership from Transition to the Transformation Decade of 2015-2024".[3] The final declaration talked about mutual commitments in the areas of governance, security, the peace process, economic and social development, and regional cooperation. Earlier, in November 2011 at the Istanbul Conference which was attended by the so-called "Heart of Asia" countries consisting of Afghanistan, China, India, Iran, Pakistan, Russia, Saudi Arabia, Turkey, UAE and all Central Asian republics, participants reaffirmed their strong commitment to a "secure, stable and prosperous Afghanistan in a secure and stable region". Apart from other things, in the context of Afghanistan, the regional countries also agreed to respect for the territorial integrity of states; non-intervention in the internal affairs of other states; dismantling terrorist sanctuaries and safe havens; disrupting all financial and tactical support for terrorism and support for the stability and peace in Afghanistan, as well as respect for Afghanistan's sovereignty, unity and territorial integrity. At the May 2012 Chicago Summit, countries belonging to the North Atlantic Treaty Organization (NATO) and International Security Assistance Force (ISAF) pledged to support Afghanistan through 2017. At the summit, the ISAF troop contributing nations and other donors pledged to contribute roughly US$ 3.6 billion annually for three years beginning in 2015 towards the development of a sustainable ANSF. Later at the Tokyo conference in July 2012, donors agreed to provide US$ 16 billion over the next four years. Moreover, the American officials also talked about working for a New Silk Road Strategy for Afghanistan.

In 2011, the Joint Coordination and Monitoring Board (JCMB), which is responsible for overall strategic coordination between the Afghan government and the international community reached an agreement to increase Afghan National Police Force from 134,000 to 157,00 and Afghan National Army from 171,000 to 195,000. Finally at the Chicago NATO summit contributing nations announced their vision for a new NATO mission to train, advice and assist Afghan forces after 2014, and a political commitment to provide funding for ANSF. The ANSF sustainment plan of 352,000 personnel has already been achieved. Although these numbers have already increased significantly, the security forces will need much more mentoring than provided so far. Due to higher rates of desertion, many more also need to be trained on regular basis. So far, Americans have provided a major share of resources for training. In fact, about 50 per cent of their committed and disbursed resources for reconstruction and development in Afghanistan have gone only to train security forces. Europeans have also contributed for police training. Apart from lack of socio-cultural understanding of new Afghan soldiers, the western training has also been very expensive. This is an area where both India and Russia could help Afghanistan. If India is able to provide some training to Afghan forces, a significant amount of resources can be freed for other development programmes.

This will also provide a major role for India in any future security scenario. Although details are not known at the moment, it is likely that a major portion of training agreed in the strategic partnership agreement will be conducted in India itself. Recently, there has also been some reports indicating possibility of Russia establishing army maintenance bases in Afghanistan. Concrete details concerning this proposal will be discussed in Moscow by end of May 2013.[4] Russia could also be supplying lot of weapons to Afghan army. The US has already purchased about 70 Russian Mi-17 helicopters for the Afghan Army.[5] Similarly, Russia is also helping NATO troops in Afghanistan by agreeing supplies through Northern Distribution Network (NDN) which pass through its territory.

Although there is a lot of media focus on security situation and issues concerning 'negotiated settlement', the economic challenge facing Afghanistan is equally serious. With declining western interest, the amount of resources available for development projects in the next decade is likely to be significantly lower than the past one decade. Experience suggests that withdrawals of international troops in other parts of the world have reduced civilian aid, with implications for economic growth and fiscal sustainability. Therefore, potential financing gaps in the budget could threaten security and recent progress made at the developmental front. According to the World Bank actual aid to Afghanistan in 2010-11 was about US$ 16 billion, about the size of the nominal GDP.[6] According to the *Asian Development Bank Outlook 2011*, the planned foreign troop pullout by 2014 may lower growth by at least 2-3 percentage points.[7] Any rapid decline in aid will severely affect growth performance and employment scenario in the country.

To offset these trends, Afghanistan has to concentrate on two things. First, it has to attract private foreign investment particularly in sectors like mining, hydrocarbons, infrastructure, telecommunications, agriculture, education, health services, etc. Secondly, for long-term sustainability, it ultimately also has to play its traditional role of facilitating trade and commerce through its territories. In both these areas, both India and Russia could play a very significant role. The Delhi Investment Summit on Afghanistan (which was perhaps a first major summit organised by a regional country on its own initiative) emphasised precisely on these points.[8] The choice of India for investment summit was also important as many Indian companies have already decided on big investments in Afghanistan. A consortium of seven Indian companies led by the state-owned Steel Authority of India (SAIL) have won a US$ 10.3 billion deal to mine three iron ore blocks in central Afghanistan. Some Indian companies are also planning to bid for copper and gold projects. There are also reports that India is also planning to build a 900 Km railway line between Iran's Chabahar port and Bamiyan province where Indian companies are planning large investments.

Similar to India, Russian contribution to Afghan reconstruction could be quite significant. Recently President Vladimir Putin while discussing current situation in Afghanistan asked his officials to prepare a blueprint for "Russia's participation in implementing and financing promising international, infrastructure, transport and energy projects" in Afghanistan and the region. He also welcomed "the desire of a number of the countries in the region to join in the Customs Union and the Common Economic Space".[9] Earlier, the Russian-Afghan Forum organised by Yuri Krupnov even talked about Russian Marshall Plan for Afghanistan.[10] In recent months there are also reports that Indian public sector giant ONGC is planning to bring Russian hydrocarbons to India via Central Asia, Afghanistan and Pakistan. If taken seriously by all concerned parties, the project has the potential to fundamentally change the energy security scenario of India (and Pakistan), offer vast new markets for Russian hydrocarbons and provide an economic cushion for Afghanistan in its decade of transformation. The proposed India-Russia hydrocarbon corridor could become a game changer in regional geopolitics and economics. It will re-energize the India-Russia strategic partnership, create solid linkages between South Asia and the emerging Eurasian Economic Union and stabilise Afghanistan economically.[11] So India-Russia cooperation could become crucial for sustainability of the Afghan economy in the long run.

**Importance of Afghanistan for India**

Strategic location of Afghanistan will always be important for India, particularly in the context of difficult India-Pakistan relations. However, importance of Afghanistan for India is much bigger than normally perceived in this narrow context. Once Afghanistan becomes stable, trade through Pakistan and Afghanistan could also alter India's continental trade. Within a few years, India's trade with Europe, CIS plus Iran, Afghanistan and Pakistan would be about US$ 500 billion annually. Even if 20 per cent of this trade is conducted through road, US$ 100-120 billion of Indian trade would be passing through Afghanistan and Central Asia.[12] With improvement in India-Pakistan relations, an important portion of Indian trade (particularly from the landlocked northern states including Jammu and Kashmir) will be moving through Pakistan and Afghanistan. With the possibility of this trade passing through Afghanistan and Central Asia, most of the infrastructural projects in the region will become economically viable. These linkages will also transform small and medium industries and agriculture in Central Asia and Afghanistan. A major impediment in realizing this potential is existing difficult relations between India and Pakistan. While looking at the regional economic dynamics, it is clear that both India and Pakistan would be paying huge economic costs for not cooperating in the Afghanistan. If trade stops in Pakistan, many road and other infrastructural projects will never become viable because of low volumes. Direct linkages between Central Asia and India will also give huge boost to all economies in the region, particularly to Afghanistan.

For many of these things to happen, various big and small projects discussed at different meetings in the last few years need clear prioritization. A recent study has clearly outlined some concrete immediate and long term measures which can soften the economic impact of military drawdown and create conditions for self sustained growth.[13] Earlier, it was thought that Afghanistan has very limited resources. The Afghanistan government in 2010 claimed, however, that the country has huge untapped mineral resources worth at least 3 trillion dollars.[14] Afghan and American officials have now repeatedly talked about the New Silk Road Strategy. Since 2005, the idea has been discussed at many academic and policy forums. This strategy is a long term vision of an international trade, transit and energy network that links Central and South Asian economies through Afghanistan.[15] This was a good blueprint for Afghanistan but unfortunately has been mixed with regional geopolitics and exit strategies from Afghanistan. Still, Afghanistan has no other option but to continuously working for this strategy. Many analysts have pointed out difficulties in implementing this strategy particularly in the context of difficult India-Pakistan as well as Pakistan- Afghanistan relations. This is true that it is difficult to imagine implementation of this policy in the present tensed political environment. However, some positive developments have taken place. The Afghan-Pakistan Transit Trade Agreement (APTTA) has been reached after years of negotiations and active US encouragement. Under the agreement, both Afghanistan and Pakistan have agreed to facilitate the movement of goods between and through their respective territories. Pakistan has allowed Afghan exports to India through Wagah and to China through Sost/Tashkurgan. Similarly, Afghanistan has allowed Pakistani trucks to reach Tajikistan, Turkmenistan, Uzbekistan and Iran through its territories. Afghan trucks can carry Afghan transit export cargo on designated routes up to Pakistani sea ports of Karachi, Qasim, Gwadar and Wagah border. At the moment, this is only a partial agreement as Afghan cargo is offloaded on to Indian trucks back to back at Wagah and trucks on return are not allowed to carry Indian exports back to Afghanistan. Despite its limited nature and serious initial problems in implementation, the agreement can seen as a major development in regional economic cooperation.[16] It has also generated interest beyond Afghanistan and Pakistan. Recently, both Pakistan and Afghanistan have decided, in principle, to include Tajikistan also into APTTA. To make this initial small project into a serious regional economic force, it is imperative to include Turkmenistan, Uzbekistan (and perhaps Iran) into the broader agreement. However, the project will be of very limited interest to Central Asian countries if traffic to India is not allowed in both the directions. Once Central Asians and India are included in the expanded APTTA, the region will be ready to take advantage from the emerging Eurasian Customs Union space within a few years.

Despite tensions at the political level, there are positive developments between India and Pakistan on trade matters. Recently, both have agreed on three agreements viz. redressal of trade grievances, mutual recognition and custom cooperation. Pakistan will allow bilateral trade through Wagah for all goods (presently restricted to 137 items). India has agreed to reduce number of items under restricted list by 30 per cent. There is also a possibility of some positive movement on provision of MFN status to India by Pakistan. While India had given Pakistan MFN in 1996, Pakistan has been refusing to do so. Once that happens, India has agreed to bring SAFTA sensitive list to just 100 items immediately. Pakistan will do so in the next five years. By 2020 peak tariff rate will not be more than 5 per cent. Both have also agreed to cooperate in investment, banking, electricity and gas trade, railways and better air connectivity. In addition, they have signed new liberalized visa regime. Within the broad context of increasing regional economic cooperation, India continue to support both the Regional Economic Cooperation Conference on Afghanistan (RECCA) as well as the "Heart of Asia" processes. In the Istanbul process, India also leads in two Confidence Building Measures (CBMs) viz. Commercial Opportunities CBM and Chambers of Commerce CBM. In a separate development two meetings of a newly established trilateral India-Afghanistan-US trilateral Dialogue have also taken place.

## Post-2014 Russian Concerns

Due to its past record, it has not been quite difficult for Russia to deal with the Afghan question. Although it has not been easy for Russia to endorse NATO decisions in Afghanistan, Still, Russia is also concerned about any failure which will immediately put Russia and Central Asia in great danger. To enter back into Afghan scenario, Russia would like to revitalize Russophile lobbies in the country[17]. Until very recently, Russian priorities in Afghanistan were ambivalent. Some people in the ruling elite were pointing towards the stalemate while others were concerned with coalition's failure and its consequences. Since 2009, however, Russia is more concerned with dangers and started strategies of cooperation with NATO.[18] So far Russia's major worry has been drug traffic emanating from Afghanistan. On this front Russia has been quite unhappy with the coalition performance. Recently, Russian president Putin remarked that "the international forces are doing almost nothing to eradicate drug production in Afghanistan and Russia's proposals in this area have unfortunately been ignored". In the post-2014 situation, Russia feels that international forces have "not yet managed to achieve a turnaround in the fight against terrorist and radical groups" and Moscow is worried about "increase in drug trafficking, trans-border crime, uncontrolled flows of refugees and migrants, and fundamentalism." Overall, President Putin feels that development in the situation in Afghanistan "is a matter of direct concern for our national security."[19]

## Indian and Russian Engagement with Central Asia

Uncertainty concerning post-2014 Afghanistan has increased significance of the Central Asian region considerably for both India and Russia. The failure of Afghanistan project poses common security challenges but any positive outcome will open tremendous economic opportunities for India, Central Asia and Russia. The Afghanistan factor is also one of the main reasons for announcing a new 'Connect Central Asia' policy by India. As outlined by the Minister of State for External Affairs E Ahmed[20] at the first India Central Asia Dialogue in Bishkek in June 2012, the new policy comprises twelve points:

- Further Strengthening political relations with the region
- Strengthening strategic and security cooperation (military training, joint research, counterterrorism cooperation, close consultations on Afghanistan)
- Stepping up multilateral engagement (SCO, Eurasian Custom Union)

- Partnership in energy and natural resources
- Straitening cooperation in the medical field
- Establishing a new Central Asian University in Bishkek
- Setting up Central Asian e-network with its hub in India
- Strengthening private partnerships in sectors like construction and iron and steel
- Reactivating International North South Trade Corridor
- Strengthening cooperation in the banking sector
- Improvement in air connectivity
- Encouraging regular academic exchanges and civil society contacts

Immediately after the announcement of this new policy, the Tajik president Emomali Rahmon visited India in September 2012 and signed six agreements. India also helped building Ayni air base in the country. Both the countries have now agreed to deepen counter terrorism cooperation and elevate the relations to a "strategic partnership". As SCO may play a bigger role in Afghanistan in any post-2014 situation, India is also hoping to get its full membership soon. Recently President Putin also asserted that Russia must strengthen security in its southern regions and work with Central Asian allies to protect itself against the threat of extremist violence emerging from Afghanistan. He outlined that "we should reinforce the security system in the strategic southern direction, including the military component. We are to use the full arsenal of preventive measures, and also the potential offered by the CSTO and the SCO".[21]

**Conclusion**

It is becoming clear that in the post-2014 phase, Afghanistan is going to face three major challenges—security, political and economic. In all three areas, enhanced Indian and Russian engagement in Afghanistan could help the country meet these difficult challenges during its decade of transformation (2015-2024). Compared to other western nations which are planning to reduce their engagement after 2014, both India and Russia may be preparing for an enhanced engagement in the country. The enhanced Indian role is based on the assessment that international support to Afghanistan will continue much beyond 2014 and there is little scope for any 'negotiated settlement' in the near future. The increased Russian engagement will be to deal with threats concerning fundamentalism, drug trafficking, cross-border crime and flow of refugees. This will be dealt both through helping stability inside Afghanistan through institution building and also from outside through coordinated actions within CSTO and SCO. Both India and Russia have clearly understood that long term stability in Afghanistan would also depend on sustainable economic growth in the country. Therefore, investment inside Afghanistan and an economic plan of linking South Asia to the emerging Eurasian integration project will be crucial. India-Russia cooperative projects in many of these areas could greatly help stabilizing post-2014 Afghanistan. As trusted and reliable strategic partners,[22] both India and Russia can easily work joint capacity building programme for the Afghan security forces and joint economic strategies for Afghanistan and the wider region.

## NOTES

1. *Report on Progress Toward Security and Stability in Afghanistan*, (United States Department of Defense Report to the Congress, December 2012), p. 1.
2. For detail of the agreement see "Text of Agreement on Strategic Partnership between the Republic of India and the Islamic Republic of Afghanistan" October 4, 2011, http://goo.gl/Prt4h
3. Bonn Conference Conclusions, Afghanistan and the International Community: From Transition to the Transformation Decade, 5 December 2011, http://www.auswaertiges-amt.de/cae/servlet/contentblob/603686/publicationFile/162662/Konferenzschlussfolgerung_engl.pdf
4. "Russia, NATO to Discuss Afghanistan Maintenance Bases" *Ria Novosti*, 27 March 2013, http://en.rian.ru/world/20130327/180287510.html

5. Fred Weir, 'Russia Going Back to Afghanistan? Kremlin Confirms it could Happen" *The Christian Science Monitor,* 1 April 2013.
6. *Transition in Afghanistan: Looking Beyond 2014*, (Washington DC: The World Bank, 2011).
7. *Asian Development Outlook*, (Manila: ADB, 2011), p. 157.
8. For details see Gulshan Sachdeva, "The Delhi Investment Summit on Afghanistan", *IDSA Comment*, 26 June 2012, http://idsa.in/idsacomments/TheDelhiInvestmentSummitonAfghanistan_gsachdeva_260612
9. Security Council Meeting of the Russian Federation, 8 May 2013, http://eng.news.kremlin.ru/news/5381/print
10. Roman Muzalevsky, "The Russia Afghan Forum: A Russian Marshall Plan for Afghanistan, *Central Asia Caucasus Analyst,* 17 June 2009.
11. For details see Gulshan Sachdeva, "India's ONGC Plans to bring Russian Hydrocarbons to South Asia" *The Central Asia Caucasus Analyst,* Vol. 15, No. 10, 2013.
12. For details see Gulshan Sachdeva, "Regional Economic Linkages" in Nirmala Joshi, ed, *Reconnecting India and Central Asia: Emerging Security and Economic Dimensions* (Washington DC, Washington: Central Asia-Caucasus Institute and Silk Road Studies Program, 2010), 115-179.
13. S. Frederick Starr, *et al., Finish the Job: Jump-Start Afghanistan's Economy-A Handbook of Projects,* (Washington: Central Asia-Caucasus Institute and Silk Road Studies Program, 2012).
14. "Mining in Afghanistan", http://goo.gl/GUqhg
15. See S. Frederick Starr and Andrew C. Kuchins, etc. *The Key to Success in Afghanistan A Modern Silk Road Strategy,* Silk Road Paper (Washington: Central Asia-Caucasus Institute and Silk Road Studies Program, 2010).
16. Gulshan Sachdeva, "Afghanistan and Pakistan Sign Trade and Transit Agreement", *Central Asia Caucasus Analyst,* Vol. 12, No. 6, 2010.
17. Marlene Laruelle, *Beyond the Afghan Trauma: Russia's Return to Afghanistan,* Jamestown Occasional Paper, August 2009
18. Marlene Laruelle, Russia's Perceptions and Strategies in Afghanistan and their Consequences for NATO," NATO Research Paper, No. 69, November 2011.
19. Security Council Meeting of the Russian Federation,8 May 2013, http://eng.news.kremlin.ru/news/5381/print

20. For details see, Keynote Address by E. Ahmed at First India-Central Asia Dialogue, June 12, 2012, http://goo.gl/Io5ah
21. Security Council Meeting of the Russian Federation, 8 May 2013, http://eng.news.kremlin.ru/news/5381/print
22. For details see Gulshan Sachdeva, "India's Relations with Russia" in David Scott (Ed) Handbook of India's International Relations (London: Routledge, 2011).

# 4
# Russia and the Asia-Pacific

*Baladas Ghoshal*

Russian foreign policy faces the dilemma of a self-perceived image and notion of a Soviet-era great power and the actual reality of a truncated and a stagnant Russian petro-state seeking to insulate itself from the forces of change, with reduced capacity in both its military and economic power, as well as in diplomatic leverage. That dilemma and the existential crisis are also evident in her policies and approaches to the Asia-Pacific region, even though it is slowly changing under new circumstances and imperatives. An important feature that influenced Moscow's approach to the Asia-Pacific region in the post-Soviet period is its failure to achieve its desired goal of integration with the West, which, of course, had always been the focus of its foreign and defence policies even under the Soviet Union. Russia's foreign ambitions have been directed almost entirely westward throughout its long history. However, even while the Soviet Union's major concern was its equation with the West, the compulsions of Cold War and its rivalry with the United States led Moscow to devote its considerable resources to gain influence and expand its reach in Asia. The collapse of the Soviet Union and the end of the Cold War changed all that, as the successor state Russia, with its devastated and devalued economy, not only witnessed its reach and leverage in Asia evaporate, but also did not find any immediate incentive to build on its past and resuscitate its relations with its erstwhile friends in Asia. The only exception, however, was India, whose relations with Moscow also experienced a lot of turbulence in the post-Soviet era and in spite its recent improvement has not reached the same level of the past. Moscow in its traumatic years of the 1990s laboured under the delusion that the West would embrace Russia, salvage its economy, flung open its arms for its entry into the European Union and even membership of the NATO. To its utter disappointment and frustration, it discovered that the West had neither any desire to fulfill its expectations, nor was prepared to give it the status that it felt it deserved. As a result, Russia failed to develop a sustainable cooperative relation with the United States. More importantly, some of Moscow's recent actions, particularly in Georgia's civil war have led to a straining of relations between Russia and the NATO and, in turn triggered a proposal of an eastward expansion of the latter to Georgia and Ukraine, a move considered by Russia as a threat to its own national security.

Moscow's response to such Western neglect was to look toward the East, particularly toward China, as a desperate attempt to find a friend who shares its hostility vis-à-vis the West equally, or even more, and who can help it to shore up its lost image, power and influence in the world, lending its foreign policy an anti-Western, particularly, anti-US stance. "China's weight and power, plus the familiar style of its authoritarian regime, make it a natural magnet for Russia's elite," writes Lilia Shevtsova, "China was a country of interest in Soviet times, but this focus diminished when Russia attempted integration with Europe. Russia later renewed its interest in China in the mid-2000s, when Russia's relationship with the West soured. There is an anti-American dimension to this partnership, but it also reflects a genuine desire in Moscow for mutually advantageous economic cooperation with Beijing."[1]

In its fight against the hegemony of the United States as the only super power, Beijing also found Moscow as an important ally and developed close political and economic relations between the two. While Russia's relations with China flourished and continue to deepen taking the form of strategic partnership, its relationship with other countries in Southeast and East Asia, even with its erstwhile ally, Vietnam failed to take off for a considerable period until very recently. Even then, it is still quite marginal, making Russia's look eastward essentially an China-centric. With other countries in the region, it had to build relations practically from the scratch. Russia's move toward the Asia-Pacific region, therefore, was essentially after-thought, and reactive to its failure to achieve its desired goal of integration with the West. However, geo-political realities, the rise of Asia together with a shift of global economic activities from the West to the East, and economic necessities of developing a backward Siberia and its Far East territories have led Moscow in recent years to focus on the Asia- Pacific region to secure its claim and position not only as an European power but also as great Pacific power. Russian experts such as Dmitri Trenin of Moscow Carnegie Center, now see the dynamic economies of Asia an opportunity for the renewal and unification of his country.[2] Russian strategic thinkers define the main goals of their foreign policy in East Asia in terms of preservation of their own national interests, development of large-scale cooperation with main global and regional actors and avoidance of confrontation, preventing an arms race in the region, and finally finding possibilities for integration into the existing system of economic growth in East Asia.[3] From its earlier reactive policy, Moscow has now embarked on a more pro-active diplomatic offensive toward the Asia-Pacific region, relying mostly on a search for markets for its weapons, oil, gas and its scientific knowledge, to change the balance of forces in the region.[4] And while relations with the West continue to dominate Moscow's foreign policy, recent developments suggest that Russian policy makers are now reassessing the importance of the Asia Pacific region.[5] In the last decade, Russia has actively engaged with its neighbours through multilateral cooperation and efforts at economic integration. At the same time, Russia has its own limitations, as realization slowly dawned, that mere possessions of resources are not enough guarantees for demand on its markets. It has to be made attractive through the creation of a friendly business environment and the development of infrastructure.

## Limitations in Russia's Look Eastward

While oil and gas remain the major Russian export basket to the Asia-Pacific countries, its share in the Russia's overall export of fuel and energy is still quite low - first of all to China, the Republic of Korea, Japan, and the United States, amounts to approximately 15 per cent of total Russian exports on international markets and less than 10 per cent of refined oil products. Exports of liquefied natural gas (LNG) to these countries also do not exceed 7 per cent out of its total export of natural gas. APR's share of Russia's exports of coal totals 23 per cent, aluminum—35 per cent, and copper—16 per cent. If Moscow has to take advantage of its available potential in its Far East region and Siberia by linking it to the Asia-Pacific markets, it has to develop the raw mineral extraction in the eastern regions that can "attract investments in infrastructure, production facilities to manufacture high value-added products, and enterprises with advanced technologies to produce engineering and construction equipment required for mining and processing enterprises."[6] Currently, the lack of development in the region has led to exodus of population from the area to major cities all over Russia that has affected the social and economic situation in these regions. To halt population exodus from the region, Russia needs to fashion a comprehensive strategy at the federal level to develop the region through "incentives for economic growth, including directed state funding, the introduction of fiscal and customs privileges, and attracting highly skilled personnel to move to these regions." The recognition for adopting such a strategy does exist in the policy circles, as in one of his first decrees after his latest inauguration ("On measures of the implementation of the foreign policy of the Russian Federation"), President Vladimir Putin declared the objective of increasing "participation in the APR integration processes with the goal of promoting the accelerated social and economic development of the regions of Eastern Siberia and the Far East, deepening equal, trust-based partnership and strategic cooperation with China, strategic partnership with India and Vietnam, and developing mutually beneficial cooperation with Japan, South Korea, Australia, New Zealand and other key nations in the Asia-Pacific region."[7] In fact, the Ministry for Development of the Far East was also established with this specific objective in mind.[8] However, implementation of these plans and programme are plagued by budget constraints, lack of a comprehensive energy strategy and immediate incentives for development as long as prices for raw material remain high and finally the centralization of resource rents and the past practice of financial equalization between the regions. The result is stunted development of Russia's Far East and Siberia. To quote Alaexander Panov, an analyst at Russian International Affairs Council:

> It is obvious that in such a vast country as Russia, applying a uniform system of business Development plans for the Far Eastern regions that are derived off of "regular, standard conditions" imply resource extraction using old technology and infrastructure. Such an approach will increase exploitation, but limit economies of scale because of insufficient investment, restrictions on foreign investors from exploring new deposits, the absence of necessary infrastructure, and underdeveloped manufacturing capacities. Innovation will suffer under this scenario.[9]

The Russian gas and oil are coming under increasing competition from other suppliers, constraining its leverage in oil and diplomacy. For example, Mozambique, Turkmenistan, Kazakhstan, Canada, and the U.S. through its exploitation of shale gas are emerging as new sources of gas, and offering it at lower prices than the Russians. Countries which have a hunger for energy are investing overseas to secure steady and sure supply of gas for their needs. China and Japan, for example, have invested billions of dollars to acquire and explore gas deposits in Africa and Latin America. In contrast, the development of Russian deposits in Siberia and Sakhalin has not progressed much for the lack of comprehensive strategy, market incentives and development of infrastructure. Even though foreign companies, especially ones from Japan and South Korea, are interested in entering the Russian Far Eastern market, including carrying out raw material and infrastructure-related projects, the uncertain business environment and practices of Russian partners of foreign companies changing the terms of contracts without prior consent or even forcing foreign partners out of projects without compensation are halting the development of the Russian Far East market.[10] Russia is also facing completion in prices of gas, as a number of foreign producers are already selling natural gas on the global market at prices below Russian rates. China has managed in late 2011 to get Turkmenistan to annually supply 65 billion cubic meters of natural gas to China—more than half of its 2010 consumption. This had given Beijing the upper hand in future price negotiations with the Russians and left its energy company Gazprom's strategy in Asia in crisis. The Russian Far East is not only producer of gas but also can become an important supplier of agricultural products, both for technical needs and for the wider food industry, for which not only foreign equipment, technologies and work force are required but also foreign investment. Again, the Russian unpredictable business environment stands in the way of such investments to flow into the country.

Nevertheless, Russian experts and commentators recognize the need for the inflow of foreign investment into the region, for that would help modernize Russian corporations and facilitate their incorporation of modern methods of management, production processes, and adherence to transparency. The money from the foreign investment would also help the Russians to modernize the transport infrastructure in the region. In fact, in June 2013, President Putin, speaking at the St. Petersburg International Economic Forum, announced ambitious plans to boost Russia's economic growth by looking to the Asia-Pacific region rather than to its traditional markets in Europe, and proposed massive investments in infrastructure, including upgrading the trans-Siberian railway to better link his country to the Pacific.[11] Moscow has also developed, over the past two decades, considerable oil and gas resources on Sakhalin Island to respond to the growing energy demands of its neighbours in Northeast Asia, and completed the construction of a major oil export pipeline across Siberia to the Pacific coast that also links to China. Most recently, it agreed to export 365 million tons of oil to China over the next 25 years. But Russia's 20 million tons in 2011 accounted for only around six percent of Chinese oil imports, well behind Saudi Arabia and Angola. Even if the latest deal goes through, it is difficult to see how Russia's market share will grow significantly given the general increase in Chinese oil exports. According to some experts, gas exports to China have proved even more difficult for Russia to pull off. Between 2004 and June 2013, the two countries concluded no less than six agreements for gas trade but have yet to reach a deal on actual deliveries.

## Russia's Pivot to Asia and the Russia-China Strategic Partnership

Fiona Hill, a Russian expert at America's Brookings Institution feels that Russia's shift in economic focus towards its Far East might sound very much like the U.S. pivot to Asia, as Russia attempts to reassert its military presence in the Asia-Pacific like the United States and other regional powers.[12] But the difference is that whereas Washington's pivot to Asia is viewed to be directed essentially against China, Moscow has gone at great length to emphasize that its primary goal is to cooperate, not compete, with Beijing. Russia denies that there is even the slightest element of trying to contain China in its regional policy. On the other hand, Putin suggested that he would like to deepen even more his country's cooperation with China.[13] He blamed the "foreign experts" of "always trying to frighten us with China." During a meeting with international journalists and analysts in the Russian Black Sea resort city of Sochi in September 2010, Putin declared: "We're not frightened. China does not worry us. China and Russia will cooperate on many questions."[14] Putin expressed his full satisfaction with the state of relations with Beijing, which too is willing to oblige Moscow for its own strategic reasons. There are of course perfectly legitimate reasons for close Chinese-Russian relations. China is the world's biggest energy consumer whilst Russia is the biggest energy provider. Trade between the two countries is booming and is now worth some $88bn per annum and is expected to exceed $100 billion in 2013. For Russia, China is already the biggest trade partner, if the European Union is not considered a single economy. In 2012, China accounted for slightly over 10 per cent of Russia's foreign trade; while the Russian share in China's foreign trade is much smaller and barely exceeds 2 per cent. Nevertheless, Russia is already turning into an important supplier of certain raw materials to China and its role will grow as Beijing is seeking to diversify sources of their supply. Chinese President Xi Jinping also made a call to expand Sino-Russian trade from the sphere of raw materials into other realms: It is rational now to stimulate developing relations not only in raw economic, but also in investment, high technologies and finances, to start cooperating not only in trade but also in joint research and manufacturing.

China is also emerging as an important investor in Russia. The chief of Gazprom Alexei Miller, was quoted as saying that China would fund a branch line of a Siberian pipeline, which would mean that Russia would deliver gas to China by 2018, helping the latter to clean up its development—switching from coal and oil to gas, and, that too at a discount. China drives a hard bargain for Russian gas and oil just as it does for Iranian oil. Russia already charges China less for the power it provides than even to Russians themselves. And China is extremely generous in making available funds to Russia, which it uses to sell oil to China. China agreed to lend Russian state-owned energy company Rosneft US$ 2 billion in exchange for a planned tripling of Russian oil exports to China. Russian oil sales to China is expected to go up to 31 million tons in a couple of decades. Russia is building a new network of oil pipelines to the Far East. China is building a massive refinery in Tianjin, which will mainly refine Russian crude. China will build roads and power plants in Russia so that Russians can mine their own coal, generate electricity and transmit it to China.

While both Russia and China try to portray their relations more in economic terms, the primary driver of ties between Moscow and Beijing is strategic. Both feel immense pressure from the world's sole "hyper power". Russia has long viewed expansion of the North Atlantic Treaty Organization (NATO) deep into Eastern Europe as an aggressive move. China now has similar concerns about Washington's militarized "pivot" to Asia and support for Japan, Vietnam, and the Philippines in their territorial disputes with Beijing. Both Moscow and Beijing have deep distrust of Washington's expanding military presence in what is perceived as their strategic backyards, and therefore, have common interests in countering the US move in the region. As a symbol of importance and priority Beijing gives to Moscow, Chinese President Xi Jinping chose to make his first official visit as President to Russia in March 2013.[15] And in July 2013, Beijing and Moscow solidified their cooperation with joint naval exercises in the Sea of Japan, another symbol of their joint cooperation in defence and security.[16] The land armies of the two countries also held a joint drill in late July in the Ural Mountains in Russia. They are engaged in the training of military personnel, and the exchange of intelligence. From the Chinese perspective, solid ties with Russia serve to counterbalance America's unilateralist ambitions. Moscow is much more concerned by Washington's strategy to strengthen its military presence and expand anti-ballistic missile systems defenses in the Asia-Pacific. Leading Russian (and Chinese) policy-makers and experts do not buy the logic of American-led missile defense system in East Asia is aimed toward Pyongyang. On the other hand, they sincerely believe that these plans are essentially a form of power projection vis-à-vis Moscow and Beijing. This was evident at the March joint press conference of Xi and Putin, who jointly expressed concerns about America's ballistic missile defense system viewed as an existential threat to their nuclear deterrents. While Russia maintains an arsenal of well over 1,000 nuclear warheads, China is widely believed to have only several hundred. In the (unlikely) event of full-scale nuclear war, Russia could almost certainly overwhelm any America's missile defense system with sheer numbers. It is not clear whether China could do the same. Thus the strategic embrace between China and Russia are driven by a shared perception of American pressure on their own backyard. Incidentally, the joint statement of the two leaders also touched on the issue of the "defeated powers" of World War II. In all probability, this was an implied message of Russian support for China in Beijing's ongoing territorial dispute with Japan with whom Russia also contests territory. In the field of defense and security, apart from large-scale military-technical cooperation, Russia and China have taken every measure to build mutual confidence by trying to build a positive image of each other at home. Russia has helped China modernize its military with large-scale supplies of weapons and technologies, and the two countries are forging close military-to-military ties.

Politically, the two countries coordinate their activities in various formats and mechanisms of political interaction, such as joint participation in the Shanghai Cooperation Organization (SCO) and BRICS and cooperation in discussing international issues in the United Nations, including regular consultations between the foreign ministries and coordination of positions ahead of important votes in the UN Security Council. Moscow-Beijing ties get solidified by their shared belief that the post-Cold War international order, designed by and for the United States, denies them their rightful place at the table, while allowing Washington to throw its weight around without regard for the interests of others. This sense of exclusion underpins their support for new institutional mechanisms like the SCO, BRICS and the Group of 20, as well as their portrayal of the U.N. Security Council as the sole legitimate arbiter of war and peace. On Syria and Iran, there is unanimity of views between the two countries' positions, and both oppose regime change through outside intervention. Russia and China believe that their cooperation in the security field is a very important contribution to peace and stability in Eurasia. China has gone at great length to allay Russia's concerns about a possible political rivalry between the two countries in the post-Soviet area, by cold shouldering attempts by some post-Soviet countries, among them Belarus, to use China as a counterbalance to Russia's influence. During Russian President Dmitry Medvedev's visit to China in 2010, Beijing actually recognized the post-Soviet region as an area of special interests and stated in a joint document its support for Russia's efforts to ensure its national interests and security in the Caucasus and the CIS as a whole. Russia has a unique place in Chinese foreign policy, for no other country in the world has the intention and the capability to cooperate with and provide benefits to China in all spheres of global interactions, be it trade, science/hi-tech, military cooperation, law enforcement, diplomacy, culture, or any other field one would care to list. Russia needs to diversify its energy and resource customer base away from Europe, capitalize on Asia's emerging markets; China needs abundant, diverse, and secure energy supplies through non-maritime sources. Central Asia is another example. China and Russia both have strong incentives to prevent terrorism and the drug trafficking in Central Asia, and they would coordinate policies through institutions such as the SCO, regardless of their respective relationships with the West. Trade is yet another example. Russia needs to stimulate the economy of the Russian Far East, while China needs to revitalize its northeastern provinces. Sino-Russian cross-border trade is one of the channels through which both sides complement each others' development needs. All of these are lasting interests that will not change regardless of the state of each country's respective relationship with the EU or the US.

## Fear of Russian Bear Strangled in the Chinese Dragon's Embrace

While Putin's China pivot enjoys overwhelming approval in the Russian expert community, but there are also skeptics who believe that his strategy is fraught with the risk that the Russian bear might one day be strangled in the Chinese dragon's embrace. Some in Russia have expressed a growing fear of Chinese expansionism and Russia's possible transformation into China's 'junior partner'. A strategic partnership between a rising China and a declining Russia would most likely result in China turning Russia into a tool of its own agenda. The asymmetry of Russian and Chinese power has not spoiled the relationship yet, but it could at some point in the future. The Russian Far East, which constitutes 40 per cent of the country's territory, has a shrinking population of 6.5 million, whereas three Chinese regions across the border have 140 million people. Many Russians fear that demographic pressures and a growing shortage of resources can prompt China to train its sights on its northern neighbor. Russians are aware of the fact that China still considers vast territories in the Russian Far East as unfairly annexed from it in the 19th century. Beijing still considers these territories as part of China's "strategic borders" that stretch far beyond its geographic border to guarantee "living space" for the country. Even while most Russian experts think that China will pursue peaceful economic and demographic expansion, but some are skeptical of Beijing's long term intentions and do not rule out the possibility of military option to secure their "living space". In June this year, Alexander Khramchihin, a Russian military analyst published a highly provocative scenario of a Chinese blitzkrieg against Russia describing how the multi-million strong Chinese army could overrun the Russian Far East and much of Siberia within only a few weeks. In recent years China has conducted several large-scale maneuvers of land forces that involved the relocation of troops across 2,000 km of its border with Russia. While Beijing has never mentioned the real reasons for such operations, experts believe that such operations could only be possible against Russia and Kazakhstan. Some Russians also believe that Beijing has short-changed Moscow when it has copied and manufactured most of the weapons it used to buy from Russia, including the Su-27 fighter aircraft, China has itself climbed to becoming the top five weapons exporters in the world. That old Russian fighter, for instance, has been reversed engineered to become the JF-17, which China has been selling to Pakistan. Pakistan takes the bulk of Chinese weapons exports.

Even while selling his idea of Russian pivot to China, perhaps Putin is also conscious of the danger of a future threat from China, but he is trying to avoid that eventuality by locking Beijing in a tight friendly embrace of economic, political and strategic interdependence that would make conflict inconceivable. As a further insurance to protect its vast land mass from any future intrusion, Russia launched its biggest unannounced snap military maneuvers in Siberia and the far eastern region along China's borders. President Vladimir Putin, who watched part of the war games, said they were the largest ever, involving 160,000 troops, 1,000 tanks, 130 aircraft and 70 ships. The land operations involved massive redeployment of troops, weapons and hardware across several time zones closer to the Russian-Chinese border, which aimed at defending the sparsely populated Russian Far East from an unnamed opponent with characteristics much like those of the People's Liberation Army. Such massive military maneuvers right near the border of China demonstrated that behind "the happy façade of overflowing friendship, Russia harbours ingrained fears of the rising giant next door, fuelled in large measure by its own weaknesses, but also by China's policies."[17] Even before this military maneuvers, the Russian Defence Ministry had taken extra efforts to beef up its forces in the East under a sweeping military reform currently under way. When Russia's seven military districts were reorganized into four commands in 2010, the Eastern District was redrawn to entrust responsibility for the entire 4,300-km border with China, making it the largest military command and it is being rearmed on a priority basis. The overhauled command and control structure of the Eastern Military District and its ability to respond to a sudden attack was put to test during the July maneuvers, which showed that Russia could accomplish a necessary force build-up on the border with China. Apart from its immediate concern about the defence of its Far East, the concept of a Russian military and naval presence in the region has yet to be worked out according to a realistic assessment of present threats to national security. Its ability to project its power in the Asia-Pacific region is quite limited until now. The Russian Pacific fleet is composed of three cruisers, four frigates and sixteen nuclear submarines. Two big state of the art French-built Mistral-class amphibious assault ships will be deployed in the Far East commissioning. Most Russian strategic experts believe that the country must avoid, at least for the time being, being drawn in the arms race that would be ruinous for this country's economy.

Some scholars feel that Russia faces a major challenge in weaving in the dual objects of its policy in the Pacific - a political partnership with China underpinning Russia's relations in the region, and a search for alternatives to its heavy dependence on Beijing and the latter's disproportionate power and economic influence in the Far East.[18] That objective can only be achieved if Russia is able to diversify its relations with other countries in the Asia-Pacific to an extent where it feels comfortable to secure an independent place for itself. Until now, Russia has not been able to achieve that position, as it has no discernible influence on security decision-making. That remains largely the purview of China, Japan, South Korea, and the United States. Notwithstanding the visit of Japanese Prime Minister Shinzo Abe to Russia in April 2013—the first by a Japanese prime minister in a decade—relations with Japan remain quite strained. The July massive Russian military exercise in the Russian Far East, even though was interpreted by many analysts, was a show of to China, obviously did not please Japan and the United States, as they were also commonly regarded as the invading enemy forces. Moscow and Tokyo have still not signed a formal peace treaty under World War II, and their territorial dispute over the Southern Kurile (known as the Northern Territories in Japan) seems as intractable as ever. Even though Tokyo and Moscow have demonstrated restraint and a readiness to search for negotiated solutions, the territorial differences between them over the Kurile Island stand in the way of a more constructive relation between the two countries. That has, however, not prevented the Japanese businesses to find a way to participate in cooperation projects in the Far East. The most significant projects with foreign capital participation in the Eastern regions of Russia have been implemented precisely in cooperation with Japan. They include Sakhalin 1 and Sakhalin 2, the construction of Port Vostochny and LNG plant in Sakhalin, the launch of automotive manufacturing enterprises in Vladivostok and the development of Yakutia coal deposits.[19] Even in the absence of a territorial settlement over the Kurile, further economic engagements between the two countries can be expected to grow, provided the Russians make the Far East region more business friendly and develops the infrastructure there. A solution to the problem of territorial delimitation between Russia and Japan is unlikely be found in the near future.

The continuing conflict between North and South Korea hinders opportunities for Russia's cooperation with South Korea, a dynamic and promising state of the critically important East Asia region and a member of the G20. Seoul hosted its 2010 summit. Although in 2008 the leaders of Russia and South Korea declared a goal of moving toward strategic partnership, they have not been able to do much, except in the economic sector, where there are some suspicions in Moscow that South Korea is striving to attain the privileged status of Russia's leading partner in Asia for the sole purpose of receiving discounted access to Russian resources.[20] Twenty years following the normalization of relations, South Korea has become the third largest economic partner of Russia in the Asia-Pacific region. The scale of cooperation continues to expand, with particular attention being paid to joint investment projects, and the accumulative value of South Korean investments in the Russian economy in 2009 totaled US $1.5 billion. However, the national strategies of the two countries do not coincide: for Russia the top priorities are stability and development, promotion of its economic interests in the region with the aim of developing the Far East; while for South Korea the top priority is the unification of Korea on its conditions. On North Korean nuclear stand-off, Russia is the least influential player in the so-called six-party talks. Indeed, its contribution has been described in the past as "more nuisance than value" by regional diplomats.[21] Russia is almost entirely peripheral to attempts to resolve the impasse between North and South. Moscow was never been able to convert North Korean leader Kim Jong Il's well-documented fondness for lengthy Russian train trips into influence over North Korean policy; and his son Kim Jong Un, the current leader, does not seem to have inherited his father's love for the Russian landscapes. In short, to quote Fiona Hill again, "Russia's pivot is not so much policy as talk. The country has been slow to diversify relations in Asia, and Asian elites—including those in China—regard Russia as neither Asian nor a credible player in the region. They believe Russia is still rooted in Europe, or at best, partly in Central Asia, and that it has little to contribute in the East beyond natural resources and weapons."[22]

## Changing Perception of Russia's Potential Role in APR

The recent change in the strategic environment in the Asia-Pacific region after Beijing's declaration of the South China Sea as a 'core' issue and its sudden assertiveness to exercise its authority through deployment of its naval resources and capabilities and its pursuance of a policy of denial to others who have claims on South China Sea for exploitation of resources, have led the countries in the region to look for friends outside the region to balance Chinese power. This has led to some kind of an arms race in the Asia-Pacific region where the countries have concentrated on building up their armed forces and increasing military spending. One-third of the world's arms imports flow into the APR countries and naval forces are rapidly being developed. China, Japan, Republic of Korea, and Vietnam are all building or buying the most advanced ships, such as aircraft carriers, destroyers and submarines. The United States has also announced its plans to significantly increase the number of its combat ships in the Pacific area, as part of 'pivot' to Asia. As a result of these developments, even Russia now finds itself sought after as an energy and military partner, particularly by Vietnam, but increasingly by a wider range of states in Southeast Asia. The resultant Russia's growing relations with Southeast Asian states, especially in energy and defense, and the development of an alternative northern shipping route to the Malacca Straits are changing perceptions of Russia's potential role in the region, as Southeast Asian states seek to balance a rising China. Beijing's assertive claims to maritime boundaries in the South China Sea have rattled America's regional partners and led Washington to deepen its security cooperation with Vietnam, the Philippines and other states whose territorial claims China disputes. Moscow has remained silent on the territorial disputes, even as Russian energy companies have signed deals with Vietnam to develop oil and gas resources in the South China Sea—in waters claimed by China. Meanwhile, Russia's defense industry is expanding its weapons sales throughout Southeast Asia, including selling advanced attack submarines to the Vietnamese Navy. To Moscow's frustration, the opening of a gas pipeline from Central Asia to China in late 2009 has enabled Beijing to take a hard line with Moscow on negotiations to build a new Russia-China pipeline. In the face of China's increased leverage vis-à-vis Moscow in gas diplomacy, Russia's push to bring Kyrgyzstan and Tajikistan into its customs union with Belarus and Kazakhstan, along with Vladimir Putin's call to establish a Eurasian Union by 2015, are expressions of its desire to limit the reorientation of the Central Asian states' economies toward China and expand its own influence. Similarly, even while Russia finds support in China for its global positions, at the regional level, Russian leaders are now seeking to enhance their country's independence of action through an increasingly varied Southeast Asian diplomacy, including traditional allies like Vietnam, but also unexpected partners such as the Philippines. In January 2012, three Russian warships visited Manila at the same time as two U.S. destroyers, first visit by the Russian Pacific Fleet to the Philippines in 96 years. Russia and Vietnam have been deepening their relations in other spheres as well. Vietnam is considering joining the Eurasian Customs Union. Russian now seems to be veering to the idea that it is not the Sino-Russian strategic partnership that will make Russia more of a player in East Asia, as Russian policymakers originally thought nearly two decades ago, but rather Russia's role in counterbalancing Chinese power in the region, via defense and energy ties with Southeast Asian states.[23]

The most important factor that will give Russia further leverage in the region, however, is the prospect of opening up of the northern shipping route, becoming more practical with climate change. Once the route is operational, Southeast Asian states believe that Russia will not only be a new source of oil for them, but will be able to lessen their reliance on shipping through the Malacca Straits and lessen their energy security fears at a time of heightened tension in the South China Sea area. Since the record low extent of summer sea ice in 2007, scientists foresee the possibility of ice-free shipping in the Arctic Ocean by the summer of 2015. Indeed, in its "Foundations of the Russian Federation's State Policy to 2020 and Beyond," Russia has made the development of a Northern shipping route a priority. New Arctic routes via Canada (Northwest Passage) or via Russia (Northeast Passage) would cut shipping times from Asia to Europe in half, compared to passage through the Suez or Panama Canals or the Malacca Straits.[24] China and Japan are among countries to have received energy supplies from this route so far. Nonetheless, seasonal variability in ice melting and a lack of ports on the Arctic routes will limit their utility in the short term, especially for container traffic.

All the above will undoubtedly allow Moscow to increase its leverage and influence in the Asia-Pacific region. In ultimate analysis, however, the effectiveness of Russian policy to its east will mainly depend on how determined its efforts will be towards the economic, social, cultural and scientific development of Siberia and the Far East. Only the recovery of the Far Eastern regions of the Russian Federation combined with consistent and targeted diplomatic activity in the

Asia-Pacific Region will allow Moscow a springboard for its integration with Asia-Pacific and create opportunities to solidify its position as a widely recognized great Pacific power.

## NOTES

1. Lilia Shevtsova. "Russia's 'Pivot' to China," *East Asia Forum*, 19 April 2013. http://www.eastasiaforum.org/2013/04/19/russias-pivot-to-china/ (Accessed April 20, 2013).
2. In his most recent book, *Post-Imperium*, Dmitri Trenin even evoked the transformative legacy of Peter the Great suggesting that: "Russia would do well to think of Vladivostok as its twenty first century capital. It is a seaport breathing openness." Quoted in Paul Richardson, "Russia in the Asia-Pacific: Between Integration and Geopolitics," *Asia Pacific Bulletin*, East-West Center, no. 150, 16 February 2012.
3. See, Vladimir N. Kolotov. "Russia's Views of the Security Situation in East Asia," Brookings Institution, September 2012. http://www.brookings.edu/research/opinions/2012/09/17-russia-east-asia-kolotov (Accessed March 23, 2013).
4. According to Kolotov, the last factor, i.e. changing the balance of force in Asia, is not yet fully used in Moscow's foreign policy. Russia has a real opportunity to change the balance of forces in the region by delivering advanced weapon system to its partners, but this tool should be used very cautiously in order to preserve peace and stability.
5. Lilia Shevtsova of Moscow's Carnegie Center argues that three clear features define Russia's foreign policy in Asia. First, the Kremlin has not learned how to operate within a multi-polar system of international relations. It has focused on one big player—China—and has neglected other countries in the region. Second, Russia's foreign policy is oriented towards internal objectives. So the ruling elite had not drawn up a consistent policy for relations with Asia as a region or with individual countries other than China. And, there is always the possibility that, as the Putin regime weakens, the Kremlin could use several Asian countries as a policy ploy to pursue a domestic agenda. Third, because Putin's foreign policy is all about political survival, it has no modernizing dimension. For these reasons, Putin's Asian fling is likely to end in mutual estrangement, disappointment and perhaps even hostility—

but Russia's relationship with China will be central to whichever scenario plays out. See Lilia Shevtsova, "Moscow's pivot to China," *Op. Cit.*

6. See Alexander Panov. "Integration of Russia into the Asia-pacific Region (2013-2020 Outlook), *Russian International Affairs Council*, 2 April 2013. http://russiancouncil.ru/en/inner/?id_4=1642#top (Accessed April 12, 2013).
7. President of Russia, "Executive Order on measures to implement foreign policy," May 7, 2012. http://eng.kremlin.ru/acts/3764 (Accessed June 4, 2013).
8. During a meeting with members of the Federation Council on September 17th 2012, Prime Minister D.A. Medvedev endorsed the proposal to apply differentiated fiscal and investment regimes for the Far East and Eastern Siberia. Speaking at the Vladivostok APEC Forum, the Minister for Development of the Far East V. Ishaev and the Governor of the Amur region O. Kozhemyako noted the importance of establishing special conditions for the development of Far Eastern regions as a necessary prerequisite for ensuring their economic recovery. Proposals have been made that would exempt all investors—Russian and foreign – from corporate taxes, property taxes, real estate taxes and VAT if they establish new enterprises during the capital cost repayment period for these projects. See Panov, "Integration.", *Op. Cit.*
9. Panov, *Ibid.*
10. To quote Andrew Kuchins, Director of the Russia and Eurasia Program, at Center for Strategic and International Studies at the Russian International Affairs Council: "The biggest obstacle for Russia will be to convince investors—Russian, Asian, other international - that this is the investment environment that you can be confident in. Because the magnitude of levels of investments that can be required for oil, gas and other natural resources development, infrastructure development around those areas are huge. It is about one of the largest capital expenditure projects in history. These investments will be paid off not in 1-2 years, but in 5-10 or 20 years, that is why it is really important to convince the international investment community that Russia is a relatively safe bet. Another issue is corruption, which is at the heart of the investment environment. It has been acknowledged many times by President Putin, and by former President Medvedev." See Andrew Kuchins. "Russia wants to have a voice in Asia," *Russian International Affairs Council*, 8 October 2012. http://russiancouncil.ru/en/inner/?id_4=888#top (Accessed June 3, 2013).

11. According to a number of economists, establishing such an area will certainly lead to China's domination, due to its economic power and orientation of ASEAN countries towards the Chinese market. As a result, China will strongly consolidate its position in the APR.

12. Fiona Hill and Bobo Lo. "Putin's Pivot: Why Russia is looking East," *Brookings*, 31 July 2013. http://www.brookings.edu/research/opinions/2013/07/31-russia-china-pacific-pivot-hill (Accessed August 4, 2013). As one of Russia's leading commentators, Vyacheslav Nikonov, pronounced when Moscow first tested out the idea of a Pacific pivot in September 2010: Given Russia's historical eastward expansion, its unique "Eurasian" geography and fusion of cultures, and the inescapable demographic and economic rise of the Asia-Pacific, the only future for Russia is as a "Euro-Pacific" power.

13. Meeting the Chinese State Councilor Yang Jiechi in the Black Sea resort of Sochi on August 16, 2013, Putin has called for across-the-board leap in Russia-China relations, including cooperation in security and defense. Recalling his meeting with his "great friend," Chinese President Xi Jinping, in Moscow earlier this year, Mr. Putin said that they had agreed to "impart a new impulse, new quality to relations between Russia and China [and] raise them to a still higher level." "This covers the economy—China ranks first in Russia's trade turnover, as well as security and international peace." The Russian leader praised the progress Russia and China had made in the sphere of defense cooperation during the meeting. "We have been successfully cooperating in the military-technical and defense spheres," Mr. Putin said, opening the meeting. "This is evidenced by the exercises that our militaries have just wound up". The Russian leader was referring to Russian-Chinese large-scale land manoeuvres that were conducted in the Russian Urals Region from July 27 to August 15 and involved 1,500 troops and more than 250 units of military hardware, including 20 aircraft and helicopters. Last year, China resumed massive purchases of Russian weapon systems, taking delivery of seven Il-76MD heavy transport aircraft and signing contracts for the supply of 52 MI-171E helicopters and hundreds of engines for its fighter jets. China has also signed framework agreements for the purchase of Russia's latest submarines, Amur-1650 and long-range fighter planes, Su-35.

14. Quoted in Fiona Hill, *Ibid.*

15. Xi promised to expand economic, military, and strategic cooperation between the two nuclear powers. Xi followed in the footsteps of his

predecessor, Hu Jintao, by traveling to Moscow soon after his ascent to the highest halls of power in Beijing.

16. Code-named Joint Sea 2013, the joint naval drills were the largest in the history of the two countries and saw the Chinese Navy's "single biggest deployment of military force in any joint foreign exercise," according to the Chinese Defence Ministry. For three days, seven Chinese and 16 Russian warships gamed off Russia's Far East with anti-pirate and search-and-rescue operations, escorting ship convoys, ship resupply, and joint anti-aircraft, anti-submarine and anti-surface vessels defenses. The manoeuvres marked a new high in Russian-Chinese defense ties and despite their non-aggressive scenario; they were clearly directed at Japan, which has territorial disputes both with Russia and China, and at the U.S. military pivot to the Asia-Pacific region. See, Vladimir Radyuhin, "Love in the Water, fear in land," *The Hindu* (Chennai), 30 July 2013. file:///D:/Russia%20%20Love%20in %20the%20water,% 20fear%20on%20land%20-%20The%20Hindu. htm, (Accessed August 2, 2013).
17. *Ibid.*
18. See, for example, See, "Territorial disputes in the APR. Interview with Alexei Fenenko," *Russian International Affairs Council*, 12 October 2012. http://russiancouncil.ru/en/inner/?id_4=908#top (Accessed March 3, 2013).
19. See Panov, *Op. Cit.*
20. See, *The Korean Peninsula: Challenges and Opportunities for Russia*, Special Report, Nautilus Institute, 7 October 2010. http://nautilus.org/napsnet/napsnet-special-reports/the-korean-peninsula-challenges-and-opportunities-for-russia/#ixzz2cfySdDnv (Accessed July 20, 2013).
21. Fiona Hill, *Op. Cit.*
22. *Ibid.* Compounding the problem, Putin has taken a particularly top-heavy approach to foreign policy, in which he and his highest officials deal personally with leaders of other countries. That kind of operation is difficult to pull off in Asia, since Putin and his inner circle have few close contacts and little expertise there. Unlike the United States, Russia does not have the presence, the capabilities or even the degree of interest to make its pivot a strategic and economic reality.
23. See, Elizabeth Wishnick. Russia: New Player in the South China Sea? *PONARS* Eurasia Policy Memo No. 260, July 2013. http://

www.ponarseurasia.org/article/new-policy-memo-russia-new-player-south-china-sea (Accessed July 30, 2013).

24. According to the *Barents Observer*, 46 ships sailed the Northern routes in 2012, compared to 34 in 2011 and 4 in 2010, and there was a 53 percent increase in total cargo transported in 2012 over the previous year. Energy products made up the largest group of cargo (including over 894,000 tons of diesel fuel, gas condensate, jet fuel, LNG and other petroleum products out of a total of around 1,260,000 tons of cargo). See, Trude Pettersen. "46 vessels through Northern Sea Route," *Barents Observer*, 23 November 2012. http://barentsobserver.com/en/arctic/2012/11/46-vessels-through-northern-sea-route-23-11 (Accessed August 5, 2013).

# 5
# Russia-India Strategic Partnership

## Multilateral Fora and Global Political and Economic Governance

*Shamma Jain*

The time-tested India-Russia friendship, spanning 65 years, is not only based on mutual trust, but it is also conflict free, enjoying the highest level of political support in both the countries. How the 'special and privileged' strategic partnership can be reshaped and leveraged to advance the two countries' global interests in the unfolding geo-political and economic architecture is a major issue that merits attention. By re-crafting the relationship with dexterity, to address the dynamics of the emerging multi-polar world, not only will the bilateral ties between India and Russia become stronger and more relevant, but the global profile of the two countries will also be enhanced further.

There is a need to leverage the distinct convergence of views between India and Russia on major issues concerning the international system, such as – the emerging polycentric world order, regard for national sovereignty, support for multilateralism, centrality of UN role on international issues of peace and security, opposition to humanitarian intervention and meddling in internal national conflicts, and creation of a balanced financial and economic global system. A broadly common, global perspective can generate a unique synergy between India and Russia, enabling them to play a more coordinated role in the international arena such as in the multilateral fora, namely the G-20, SCO (Shanghai Cooperation Organisation),

RIC (Russia, India and China) and BRICS (Brazil, Russia, India, China and South Africa). This would enhance the shared approach between India and Russia and also open avenues for joint future endeavours.

## G-20

With the G-20 accounting for 90 per cent of the global GDP and 80 per cent of international trade, it is a key platform for countries like India and Russia to address economic and financial issues of mutual concern and systemic significance. Signalling the rising influence of emerging economies in global economic multilateralism, it can help reshape the global economy, pursuing new models for more equitable development and inclusive global growth. India supports the key objectives of the Russian G-20 Presidency during 2013, particularly the proposal for increased financing for long-term sustainable investment growth and employment generation. In this context, it is relevant to examine how BRICS can make a positive contribution. India recognises the urgency to implement the 2010 IMF Governance and Quota Reform. To enhance G-20, the growing weight of BRICS and the voice of sub-Saharan Africa and other developing countries must be represented at G-20.

The reform of the international monetary system, reshaping of the IMF's governance structure to make it more legitimate and representative, successful conclusion of the 2001 Doha Round, based on its developmental mandate, and the long awaited UN reform, are some of the key areas that can render the global political and economic governance more responsive to contemporary global challenges.

India is showing interest to work closely with Russia in contributing to the reform of the global financial architecture. The two countries can co-ordinate their responses at the level of the Sherpas' and the Finance Tracks. As the Sherpas carry out important planning, negotiation and implementation tasks regularly for non-economic and financial issues; a link between India-Russia Sherpas would be useful. The same approach within the Finance Track can be developed. India and Russia are close partners and have much to gain by building cohesive responses on the financial agenda of G-20. It is in the interest of both India and Russia to bolster the ascent of emerging powers in the global economy and within G-20 vis-à-vis the core interests of G-7.

## Shanghai Cooperation Organization (SCO)

India, which currently holds an observer status in the six-nation SCO, aspires to become a full member. The Central Asian region constitutes India's extended neighbourhood. It is a region vital to energy supply, and regional security and stability that will assume more significance in the post-2014 scenario. Political uncertainty in Afghanistan after 2014 may likely exacerbate the security challenge for Russia in its Southern buffer zone of Central Asia, and for India, a fragile security situation or a spike in instability in Afghanistan and Central Asia will have serious repercussions. During the 12th SCO Summit held in Beijing in June 2012, Afghanistan featured as the top agenda for discussions.

India is willing for a 'larger and more constructive role' in the SCO as a full-fledged member. As Russia and China, the two leading members of the SCO, are interested in a greater SCO role in Afghanistan, India's membership will bolster the grouping's involvement in the security and economic reconstruction in a significant manner. At the same time, India's 'Connect Central Asia' policy, which can open up huge economic opportunities for India, Central Asia and Russia, will also get a fillip. India's expansive engagement in Afghanistan's multi-sectoral development – infrastructure projects, power stations, solar electrification, telecommunication restoration, agriculture, public health, education, human resource development or training and capacity building programmes for Afghan national security forces – can be leveraged by the SCO, especially Russia, which is interested in undertaking development projects in Afghanistan. The regional security being of foremost importance, India has already initiated a dialogue with the Regional Anti-Terrorism Structure (RATS), the SCO's counter terrorism body, based in Tashkent. As the RATS Council-members inked agreements at the March 2013 meeting in Tashkent to enhance internet security and "to combat the use or potential use of computer networks for terrorist, separatist and extremist ends", India stands ready for cooperation in the combat against cyber terrorism.

There is apprehension in some strategic quarters that India's bid for membership is being stymied by China's strong influence in the SCO. The Central Asian States, while being politically anchored in the Soviet past, are increasingly being tied to China in the economic sphere. Some analysts also contend that Pakistan, which is pushing for full membership of the SCO through China, may trigger conflicting dynamics within the organisation, once admitted. Having provided sanctuary to many of the terrorist outfits and radical elements, operating in the SCO member states, including in Xinjiang province of China, what role does Pakistan promise to play in the SCO is an important factor in the long run.

### RIC (Russia-India-China)

The world's three largest continental-sized nations have been operational as the RIC since 1996. The fora is hinged on a convergence of broad political objectives, of its members such as opposition to unilateralism, promotion of pluralistic democratic order, support to a multi-polar system, upholding the primacy of the UN in resolving crises, and the principles of non-intervention in internal affairs of sovereign states. The political goals of the BRICS and the RIC are largely similar, but the RIC, with its Asian identity, seeks trilateral cooperation and coordination of policies on an array of global political issues. The impressive long menu of the areas it covers – ranging from regional peace, security and stability, WMD (Weapon Mass Destruction) proliferation, trans-national organised crime, illicit drug trafficking, natural disasters to financial and economic de-stabilisation, food shortages and climate change, etc. – does not, however, imply that the three members have congruent worldview or seek promotion of each other's interests in these areas.

In an era of regional and sub-regional fora, dialogue structures and multilateral diplomacy, the RIC has a role to perform in the

Asian context. It serves as a mechanism for a regular exchange of views, and implementation of joint activities in areas of mutual interest. The RIC Foreign Ministers, who held their 11th Round of Meeting in Moscow in April 2012, reiterated the need for cooperation among themselves within the framework of G-20, BRICS and the East Asian Summit. With its members connected within BRICS and SCO, RIC has the potential to gain more relevance in the regional strategic architecture.

Terrorism is one of the major concerns to all three members of the RIC. Pakistan has been the constant source from which the threat has been emanating such as the wave of terrorist attacks in Central Asia and the Uyghur extremism. India, that has been fighting terror since the late 1980s, needs strong regional and global partners to root out this scourge. Hence, RIC can be a platform to mitigate the issue together. Another priority area for the RIC to cooperate and undertake joint developmental activities is the post-2014 Afghanistan. India, with its extensive engagement in the development of Afghanistan, with which it has a strategic partnership, can be a useful partner in this context.

Despite the close cooperation between India and Russia, some concerns have been raised in the Indian strategic community. Russia has repeatedly recognised India's prominent role in the region and sees its own interest in consonance with India's interests; in this context, there are a number of questions which need to be addressed. (a) Would Russia be able to nudge China towards a more friendly approach to India? (b) Would Russia be able to act as a balancing factor to soften China's stand towards India within BRICS as well as SCO? (c) As some of the Russian strategists have projected, a US-China-India triangle as determining the global strategic architecture, does Russia consider it crucial to lend stronger support to India at SCO, RIC and BRICS? (d) The growing relationship between Russia and Pakistan, and their membership of the "Dushanbe Four" (which includes Afghanistan and Tajikistan) constitute an additional factor for comprehending the political state of play in the Af-Pak area. (e) Is Pakistan's well-documented role in aiding and abetting the radical elements and terrorist groups of concern to Russia and, if so, how does Russia seek to address this challenge? India and Russia can have convergences to develop strategic worldviews and counter-terrorism policies.

## BRICS

The BRICS, representing 25 per cent of global GDP and 43 per cent of world's population, is emerging as a new model for international relations that seeks to pursue a different trajectory for growth, stability and security. Although substantially diverse, the five largest economies in their respective regions, following a comprehensive long-term agenda and specific concrete reforms in the short-term, have emerged to represent a challenge to the existing economic and political system, led by the US and other advanced western nations.

Since India and Russia represent the strongest bilateral ties within the BRICS, it is significant that the two countries try to hinge their strategic partnership on a firm economic foundation. Unless the economic and commercial dimension of their relationship is strengthened, the political proximity in the absence of an economic cementing force may lose dynamism. The BRICS Business Council offers an additional platform to the private sector in the two countries. India and Russia should play an active role in the development agenda of BRICS. BRICS, as a new paradigm for international relations, is engaging in multi-sectoral development, with emphasis on the areas of food, pharma and health, S&T and energy. Joint ventures such as food, pharma and health etc in the other developing countries can be another area of collaboration between India and Russia

The issues concerning the global economy, international and regional security, and reforms of the global governance system are some of the key macro issues questioning the validity of the obsolete global financial and economic architecture which was discussed during the Durban Summit of 2011. The reassertion of the primacy of UNCTAD over the IMF and WTO, the setting up of a New Development Bank in near future, the development of critically important infrastructure in the Emerging Market and Developing Countries (EMDCs) and coordination in the areas of international trade, in order to foster more equitable development, inclusive global growth and global economic stability are the highlights of BRICS' recent agenda, which both India and Russia support. The BRICS has expressed its resolve to combat unemployment, check the underlying causes of increased volatility of capital flows, currencies and commodity prices, which exercise a destabilising effect on the economies of developing countries.

As the emergence of BRICS exemplifies the shift of economic and political power from the West to the emerging world, the foremost challenge for the BRICS countries lies in sustaining their economic growth that might slowdown and undermine their economic might, and affect their political and diplomatic heft. At the same time, a single dominant economy of a member country within BRICS, outranking all the other four economies combined, can have deeper repercussions. The organisation, as some opine, runs the risk of becoming a platform for expanding the influence of that single dominant economy. Hence, efforts should be geared to ensure that the BRICS becomes a new axis of global economic might, strengthening the joint voice of all five members equally.

The issues of mutual interest to India and Russia can be identified as (a) How to advance the intra-BRICS economic linkages, in view of its member countries' economic dependence on those very countries that the BRICS is seeking to become an alternative to? (b) How to ensure that the BRICS does not become a platform for promoting the economic preponderance of a single member country, particularly when the intra-BRICS trade and commercial ties are weak, except one member country having substantial trade relations with all others? (c) Given the comprehensive political agenda of BRICS, as unveiled at the 5$^{th}$ BRICS Summit 2013 in Durban, India and Russia can consult and coordinate their positions on various political challenges more closely. In fact, India, Russia and China can exert their influence, as the BRICS members, at the international fora, given their concern over the post-2014 Afghanistan and regional stability along with other related-issues of religious extremism, terrorism, trans-national crime and drug trafficking.

For the successful deliverance of the multilateral foras in global development and stability, building partnership between India, Russia and China is crucial. India is observing closely the growing proximity between Russia and China. How Russia perceives China's role globally, including in multilateral fora, and the areas of convergence and concern, is a subject of strategic significance to India.

# 6
# India Russia Defence Cooperation

*Vijay Sakhuja*

The 2000 Declaration on Strategic Partnership between India and Russia defines the contours of the bilateral relations and both countries have developed common understanding on a host of issues including convening of annual Summit level meetings, regular bilateral political and foreign office consultations on issues of mutual concern, closer cooperation at the United Nations, including its specialised agencies and institutions, at other international and regional forums and joint initiatives on key international and regional issues. In the military domain, India and Russia have a robust defence and military-technical cooperation with a long-term agenda for military collaboration. Both sides are also committed to deepening service-to-service contacts that envisage joint exercises, port calls and military exchanges.

Since the days of the Soviet Union, Russia has been a source of military hardware for the Indian armed forces and has supplied high-end military equipment. The military cooperation equipment is also significant from the perspective that Soviet Union emerged as the trustworthy supplier of military equipment whenever India was subjected to sanctions by the western governments. It is estimated that nearly 70 per cent of Indian military inventory is of Soviet/Russian origin. Between 1960 and 2000, Russian military sales to India totalled US$ 35 billion.

After the disintegration of the Soviet Union, New Delhi and Moscow continued to enjoy good political and diplomatic relations. Russia remained an important source of military hardware but India had difficulty in securing the supply lines of spares since the factories/

store houses were located in new states of the erstwhile Soviet Union. India also had difficulty in identifying the production sources and all requirements of spares had to be made to Russia. This led to high product costs, long delays in supply and keeping much equipment out of use which had adverse impact on the military preparedness of the Indian armed forces.

The bilateral military cooperation progressed smoothly until 2008 when the two sides were confronted with the negotiations on the price escalation of the aircraft carrier from initially assessed as US$ 1.5 billion (US$ 900 million for refit and US$ 600 million for MiG-29K fighter jets, and Kamov surveillance and anti-submarine warfare helicopters) to US$ 2.3 billion.

Notwithstanding that, political exchanges have continued and both sides acknowledge the 'multifaceted bilateral cooperation' and the 'enduring bond of friendship, which has strong historical roots'. During his visit to India for the 13th Annual Summit in December 2012, President Vladimir Putin impressed on the importance of bilateral relations and stated that 'deepening friendship and cooperation with India is among the top priorities of our foreign policy. India and Russia show an example of responsible leadership and collective actions in the international arena'.

## Military Technical Cooperation

In 1995, India and Russia established the India-Russia Inter-Governmental Commission on Military Technical Cooperation (IRIGC-MTC). It is an apex coordinating body for planning long-term military acquisitions and joint development of military projects by India and Russia. It is co-chaired by the defence ministers of the two sides, both meet annually and the venue alternates between New Delhi and Moscow. The first phase of the IRIGC-MTC spanned 1995 and 2010, there were as many as 200 joint projects. Significantly, Russia has not established such an arrangement with any other country and this understanding is unique to India. Under the IRIGC-MTC, India has acquired a variety of military hardware including multirole air-superiority fighters, stealth frigates, obtained technological knowhow for building a nuclear submarine and the lease of nuclear submarine from Russia.

In 2009, India and Russia agreed to expand the mandate of the IRIGC-MTC by another 10 years till 2020. Joint projects during this period include development of hypersonic version of Brahmos cruise missile, multi-role military transport aircraft and fifth generation fighter aircraft. There are also plans for the serial production of T-90S main battle tanks in India under transfer of technology. It is hoped that these would contribute significantly to the development of India's military industrial complex and also provide India access to cutting-edge military technology.

The IRIGC-MTC remains the bedrock of the current bilateral military cooperation and India has made big ticket purchases from Russia. As noted earlier, nearly 70 per cent of India's military hardware is of Russian origin and dwarfs other suppliers such as Britain, France, Israel and the United States.

### Russia Military Hardware and Indian Armed Forces

A cursory look at the inventory of the Indian Army shows that Russian/Soviet origin military hardware has dominated the inventory. Nearly 70 per cent of the armoured vehicles such as the T-54, T-55, T-72 tanks including the amphibious PT-22 and PT-76 are of Soviet/ Russian origin. Similarly a host of artillery guns, multiple launch rocket system, Anti-Aircraft Artillery and other hardware have their origins in Soviet Union and Russia.

Likewise, the Indian Navy's experience with Soviet/Russian military hardware dates back to the late 1960s. Bulk on the Indian Navy submarines, both conventional and nuclear, are of Soviet/ Russian origin. India also acquired Kashin class destroyers, Petya class antisubmarine corvettes and Osa class missile boats that were instrumental in bombarding Karachi harbour in 1971. In the1990's, India acquired Kilo class 877 EKM from Russia and in 1997, India placed orders with Russia for three Krivak III class frigates (Talwar, Trishul and Tabar) built in Russia. These were followed by three more vessels of the same class (Teg Tarkash and Trikand) are equipped with Brahmos, a jointly developed missile.

As far as nuclear submarines are concerned, in 1988, India acquired a nuclear submarine on lease from the Soviet Union and commissioned it as the *Chakra*. In 2010, India acquired on lease for 10 years an Akula-II class nuclear attack submarine which has also been named INS Chakra. The indigenously built nuclear submarine INS Arihant launched on July 26, 2009 in Vishakhapatnam has a large component of Russian technology.

As noted earlier, the 44,570-tonne Russian aircraft carrier Admiral Gorshkov, renamed INS Vikramaditya is equipped with 12 MiG-29K fighter jets and 6 Kamaov helicopters aircraft. The Project 17 (P17) Shivalik class is an enlarged and modified version of the Russian P1135.6 Krivak III Class stealth frigates built in collaboration between the Indian Naval Design Bureau (NDB) and Russia's Severnoye Project Design Bureau.

Like the navy, the Indian Air Force inventory has a variety of aircraft of Russian origin. About 80 per cent of the warplanes and their various modification variants are of Soviet and Russian make. These include the MiG-21, MiG-23, MiG-25R, MiG-27, MiG-29 and Su-30MKI. Over 50 per cent of Indian military transport aircraft including Il 78 midair refuelers are of Soviet/Russian origin. The helicopter fleet of the Indian Air Force is predominantly of Russian Origin.

In December 2012, it was announced that India and Russia have signed arms deals worth US$ 3 billion including US$ 2.2 billion, for license production for 42 Sukhoi Su-30 fighter jets. Under the agreement, Russia will deliver technical kits to the Hindustan Aeronautics Limited (HAL) to assemble in India and another contract worth US$ 1.3 billion for the delivery of 71 Mil Mi-17 military helicopters.

## Joint Military Projects

India and Russia have graduated from a simple buyer-seller

relationship to joint research, development and production of military equipment. One of the success stories of their cooperation is the development and production of the supersonic Brahmos cruise missile. The joint venture called Brahmos Aerospace is between the Defence Research and Development Organisation, India and Federal State Unitary Enterprise "NPO Mashinostroyenia" (NPOM), Russia. The Brahmos missile derives its name from two great rivers, the Brahmaputra of India and the Moskva of Russia signifying the convergence of the technical capability of the two countries. In 2007 it was announced that about 3,000 missiles would be produced and one-third of these will meet Indian armed forces requirements and also satisfy Russian and Indian contractual obligations. The balance 2,000 missiles will be offered for sale worldwide.

The success of the Brahmos Aerospace project provided the necessary impetus to both sides to explore newer vistas for joint design and development of other military hardware. Under an agreement signed in 2005, India and Russia decided to jointly develop fifth generation fighter aircraft (FGFA) jet. The joint venture is between Sukhoi's KNNAPO aircraft plant in Komsomolsk-on-Amur and the HAL, India. The Russian Air Force plans to induct the FGFA from 2015 and India would acquire about 250 aircraft.

The US$ 700 million project to produce multi-role transport aircraft (MRTA) is another example of joint venture between the two sides. In December 2006, HAL, Ilyushin Design Bureau of Russia and the Irkut Corporation of Russia (major investor to bear 40 per cent of project costs) agreed to manufacture the MRTA. The aircraft will be produced in India at HAL, Kanpur.

Interestingly, an Indian entrepreneur has emerged as an important stakeholder in the India-Russia military cooperation. In 1995, Krasny Marine Services Pvt. Ltd. (KMS) was established to render customised technical and logistic support to the Indian Navy, Indian Coast Guard, public sector Shipyards and Defence Research and Development Organisations. The agency is manned and managed exclusively by officers and technicians retired from the Indian Navy and defence shipyards. In 1998, KMS established its avionics division at Goa for repair and servicing of Russian origin aircraft and became the first

Indian company to be accredited by the Centre for Military Airworthiness and Certification (CEMILAC).

## Joint Exercises

Joint military exercises form an important component of bilateral military cooperation. Russia and India have institutionalised the Indra series of naval exercises and these have been held on regular basis. In 2005, during the Indra 2005 the Russian Defence Minister Sergei Ivanov was present to observe the joint naval exercises which included large anti-submarine ships Admiral Tributs and Admiral Panteleyev, the flagship missile cruiser Varyag, the ocean tanker Pechenega and the tugboat Kalar. A nuclear submarine of Project 09710 'Samara' pennant number K-295 from Kamchatka too had joined the manoeuvres. Indra 2005 also included air-ground phase aimed at counter terrorism on land and was held in Rajasthan involving the troop from Russia's 76th Airborne Division and the Indian 50th Airborne Brigade. Indra 2007 and Indra 2009 were held in the Pacific Ocean and the Arabian Sea, respectively. Though not structured as Indra series of exercises, INS Trishul and RFN Pyotr Veliky, a Russian nuclear-powered guided-missile cruiser carried out PASSEX in August 2010 in the Arabian Sea.

Interestingly, Russia has also watched with immense interest the growing frequency and complexity in the Malabar series of exercises between the Indian and the US Navy. Russia would very much like to engage the Indian Navy more often but is constrained due to its limited deployment in the Indian Ocean. According to the director of the Center for Indian Studies at the Institute of Asian Studies, "Military exercises are an integral component of the bilateral relations between sovereign states in today's world. The zero-sum game is long gone. Given current realities, India-US cooperation and active India-Russia cooperation are not mutually exclusive".

## Issues of Diversification

It is evident from the above discussions that there is an overwhelming dependence on Russian origin military hardware by the Indian military establishment and there are critics of the Russian equipment. For instance, it has been observed that 'over-reliance on Soviet military hardware had allowed India to postpone developing a self-reliant indigenous defence industry...the dependence on Russian weapons over 30 years was a serious strategic defect'. Some have even argued that 'although the import of Soviet weapon systems has been of immense benefit, there have been persistent problems of maintenance and support". It has also been noted that 'Domestic failure to develop sophisticated and wide range of military equipment is compelling India to sign defence agreements which will bind New Delhi with the US for a long time to come'. Indeed there is some discomfort in some quarters about the quality of Russian equipment, Russia's ability to provide product support over its life-cycle and the high trajectory of the India and US relationship.

## Transformation in Indian Strategic Interests

In the 21st Century, India exudes greater confidence and is investing significant technological and fiscal resources to develop indigenous military R&D base including related industrial complex. In the past, India's military industrial sector has been largely dominated by state enterprises. Economic liberalisation and opening up the Indian military industrial complex to the private sector has given opportunity to other potential suppliers of military hardware including western military Inc. to invest in the development of India's military R&D. These initiatives have enhanced the possibilities for joint development projects, transfer of technology and even export to international customers. There is a strong belief in India that it would not like to be caught in a situation where it has placed 'all the eggs in one basket' and in this case Russia.

In the last two decades, Indo-U.S. relations have witnessed a phenomenal growth that covers a host of bilateral engagements covering political, economic, technology and security. These have spawned new joint ventures between government and commercial enterprises. Perhaps the most significant aspect of the India-US relationship has been the nuclear deal facilitating transfer of the US civil nuclear technology and also the US role in NSG waiver for the supply of nuclear fuel.

In recent times, the US has emerged as a significant supplier of military hardware to India. India's shopping list includes: (a) Thales-Raytheon Systems AN/TPQ-37 (V) 3 Fire finder artillery radar valued at US$ 3.29 billion; (b) INS Jalashwa and six second-hand UH-3H Sea King helicopters; (c) Six C 130 J Super Hercules military transport aircraft; (d) 10 Boeing C-17 advanced airlift aircraft for over US$ 2.4 billion; and (e) P-8 I long range maritime reconnaissance aircraft order for US$ 2.1 billion.

At another level, the Indian government has changed its Defense Procurement Policy (DPP) which encourages global tenders and provides greater transparency in the competition process. The DPP has been further modified and the thrust is on self-reliance through indigenisation which would further add to the competitive arms acquisition process. The new guidelines encourage foreign arms manufacturers to develop partnerships with Indian companies both public and private and this could be a good way for Russia to remain a major supplier of military hardware to the Indian establishment.

## Conclusion

It is true that the India-US strategic partnership did generate some discordant notes in the bilateral relations between India and Russia. However, the two sides were quick to seek remedy which is evident from the current state of political and diplomatic exchanges. Both sides have conveyed to the international community that the time-tested relationship has deep foundations and they respect each other's national interests.

The military cooperation has graduated from simple sale of weaponry from Russia to India to joint development of new technologies, weapon systems and platforms. India stands to benefit immensely from Russian military market and these can act as catalyst for the augmentation of India's military industrial complex. Similarly, the partnership is beneficial for Russia too in more ways than one.

This is an updated and modified version of an earlier paper by the author, published in the 'Indian Foreign Affairs Journal', Volume 5, No. 3 (July-September 2010), entitled "A Catalyst for India's Military Industrial Complex" as a part of a debate on "India, Russia and the Shift in Global Balance of Power", and is published with grateful acknowledgement and their concurrence.

# Section II

## Perceptions on Regional Issues

# 7
# Central Asia

## A Platform for India-Russia Cooperation

*Angira Sen Sarma*

International politics has undergone sea-changes since the disintegration of the erstwhile Soviet Union. With the changing international milieu, India-Russia relations have also witnessed several ups and downs but the relationship has withstood the test of time.The year 2012 marked the 65th anniversary of the diplomatic relationship between India and Russia. The signing of the 'Declaration on the India-Russia Strategic Partnership' in 2000 and subsequently elevating the strategic partnership to the level of 'Special and Privileged Strategic Partnership' in 2010, reflects the qualitative changes that has taken place in the bilateral relationship. An important aspect of the relationship is the common perceptions the two countries share on various international issues.

Among many areas, the regional landscape provides ample opportunities for enhancing India-Russia cooperation. Here, the Central Asian region holds a special place. India and Russia enjoy a deep historical connection with the region. Central Asia provides a platform for India and Russia to expand their "traditional spheres of cooperation" as the two countries would like to see a "stable and peaceful" Central Asia.[1] It is not to suggest that the interests of the two countries do not conflict with each other in the region.

This chapter attempts to explore the possibilities of Central Asia emerging as an area for India and Russia to cooperate. The chapter outlines a few areas of joint initiatives between India and

Russia in Central Asia.The Shanghai Cooperation Organization (SCO) is an area that holds immense potential for India, Russia and the Central Asian countries to work together. Endowed with rich natural resources, the Central Asian States (CAS) especially the hydrocarbon rich countries of the region have witnessed intense competition among countries to gain access to the region's resources. Although there are opportunities for India and Russia to cooperate in the Central Asian energy sector, one cannot rule out the competition between the two countries. The future of joint partnership in the energy sector depends on how the two countries address the issue and also on the policies of the CAS. China, has emerged as an important economic player in the region. India and Russia are carefully watching the growing presence of China in the region. Will the increasing influence of China provide grounds for India and Russia to look for avenues of cooperation in the region? Stability of Central Asia is critical to both countries. The deteriorating situation in Afghanistan and the impending draw down of the international forces from Afghanistan in 2014 are concerns looming large over CAS, India and Russia. Will the coming days see substantial cooperation among these countries in tackling the challenges emanating from Afghanistan?

## Why Central Asia is Critical?

Before highlighting the specific areas where India and Russia can cooperate in the Central Asian region, it is worthwhile to see the significance the region holds for India and Russia. The two countries have their own interests in the Central Asian region.

Even during the Soviet period, India had contact with the region, a legacy of Indo-Soviet friendship. With the emergence of five sovereign states post disintegration of the Soviet Union, the region witnessed several changes. The CAS's interaction with the international community increased after 1991. Russia and India also had to formulate their policies towards the region in accordance with the new realities in the region.

Russia remains an important partner of the CAS. Its relations with these republics hold a critical place in Russia's foreign policy. The region holds economic and strategic significance for Russia. The 2013 Concept of the Foreign Policy of the Russian Federation reflects the importance the Commonwealth of Independent States (CIS) hold for Russia. It notes "priority areas of Russian foreign policy include the development of bilateral and multilateral cooperation with the CIS Member States, further strengthening of the CIS as a basis for enhancing regional interaction among its participants who not only share common historical background but also have great capacity for integration in various spheres".[2] Russia's economic interests in the region are intricately linked with the larger geopolitics of the region.[3]

The strategic and economic significance of the region for India is immense. Of the five CAS, three countries are rich in hydrocarbons. The abundance of hydrocarbon reserves in the region and the growing demand for safe and reliable sources of energy supply in India make the region critical for meeting India's energy demands. The region is geo-strategically located. Three of the five CAS (Tajikistan, Turkmenistan and Uzbekistan) share border with Afghanistan. A stable Central Asia is critical for India's national security and in protecting India's energy and economic interests in the region. It is argued that "India would have to focus on greater involvement with Central Asia and cooperate with countries which will be threatened as much as India if the forces of terror were to re-emerge....it is imperative for India to intensify its strategic co-operation with Russia and the Central Asian states in the security sphere".[4]

## Areas of Cooperation

The SCO, an emerging regional group in the Eurasian region, holds immense potential for India to deepen its ties with the region.[5] While Russia is a founder member, India is an observer in the group. India was included as an observer in 2005. India has now shown interest in upgrading its membership as a full member in the Organisation. India's new interest in the Organisation is reflected in Foreign Secretary's statement in November 2010:

> "India attaches great importance to Shanghai Cooperation Organisation, most of the members of which belong to our extended neighbourhood. India has played a constructive and important role in SCO as an observer and has consistently articulated its desire to play an expanded and more meaningful role on the SCO platform. We value the role of the SCO in bringing security, stability and development to our region and stand ready to contribute more to the SCO. The SCO can play a critical role in countering terrorism through collaborative efforts and a greater profile in Afghanistan."[6]

SCO still continues with the moratorium on inclusion of new members started in 2006. Once SCO opens its door to new members, India is a potential candidate. With membership in the SCO, India would get an opportunity to share a common platform with the five CAS and with some of the important neighbours of the region like Russia and China.[7] SCO would give India for the first time an opportunity to be a member of a regional group in Central Asia.[8] Russia has supported India's candidature in the SCO. As an influential member in the group, Russia's support holds importance for India. Some scholars in Russia view India's membership could "make a significant contribution to the development of Central Asian countries and help diversify their external economic relations".[9] In general, the CAS has also welcomed India's membership in the SCO.

In future, if India is included as a member, the group could provide a common platform for cooperation among India, Russia and CAS. Membership in SCO would give India access to information gathered by the Tashkent based Regional Anti-Terrorism Structure (RATS).[10] The call for creation of an 'energy club' within SCO as suggested by Russia in 2007, if realised, would give India greater opportunity to access the region's energy resources.[11]

If membership is opened to India, other observers like Pakistan would also be included. China has always supported Pakistan's candidature and has been opposed to India. Prospects for cooperation could be marred by the China-Pakistan nexus trying to thwart India's interests, which has to be addressed carefully to avoid unpleasant developments.[12]

### *Energy Dynamics*

Three of the five CAS are rich in hydrocarbon reserves. Russia remains an important player in the region's energy sector. Until recently, India had no place in the region's energy sector. With India getting 25 per cent stake in the Satpayev block in Kazakhstan in 2011, India finally stepped in the region's hydrocarbon sector. Russia is still a key player in the region's energy sector. In future, will it be possible for India and Russia to participate in joint explorations of oil and gas fields in Central Asia? Any such project has to be mutually beneficial for all the concerned countries. Market forces and competition involved in these projects have to be carefully considered.

Tapping the hydroelectric potential of the region could be another potential area of cooperation between India and Russia. Tajikistan and Kyrgyzstan possess rich water resources. The Central Asia South Asia Electricity Transmission and Trade (CASA 1000) project aims to transmit electricity from Central Asia to its southern neighbours: Pakistan and Afghanistan. The project is in its preliminary stage, but it is worthwhile to explore possibilities of extending the project to India. Here, Russia as a member country could facilitate inclusion of India in the project.

### *China as a Factor*

Russia and China are two main players in the region with own stakes to preserve their interests in the region. The two pipelines carrying Central Asian oil and gas to China have strengthened China's position in the region. Now, no country can ignore the enormous influence China enjoys in the region. In future, the pursuit by China and Russia of their respective economic interests in this region would create rift between the two countries.[13] China's growing influence also affects India's long-term energy interests in the region. India suffered a major setback in 2005 after India's ONGC lost out to China's CNPC to acquire PetroKzakhstan. In future, will China factor be a ground for cooperation between India and Russia in the region? It is also important to see whether SCO can emerge as a platform for cooperation among Russia, India, China and CAS? These are complex issues that would play a crucial role in the geo-politics of the region.

### *Other Areas*

Another potential area of cooperation is the Customs Union. The December 2011 Joint Statement between India and Russia mentions: "the sides decided to jointly study the possibility of a Comprehensive Economic Cooperation Agreement between India and the Belarus-Kazakhstan-Russia Custom Union".[14] In India's 'Connect Central Asia' policy, India has expressed its willingness to "step up multilateral engagement with Central Asian partners using the synergy of joint efforts through existing fora like the SCO, Eurasian Economic Community (EEC) and the Customs Union. India has already proposed a Comprehensive Economic Cooperation Agreement to integrate its market with the unifying Eurasian space".[15] The agreement on FTA/CECA hold huge opportunities but there are glitches that have to be addressed like "harmonisation with WTO rules, country of origins norms, impact on other FTAs etc".[16]

One of India's major handicaps in establishing vibrant trade with the CAS is the lack of direct access to the region. Hence, another significant area where India-Russia cooperation mirrors in the Eurasian space is the international transport corridor: International North-South Corridor (INSTC).[17] The INSTC is a project, once operational would connect South and Central Asia. India was one of the original signatories of the INSTC agreement signed in 2000 at St. Petersburg. The two other original signatories were Russia and Iran.[18] The Corridor will make trade between Asia and Europe time saving and cost effective. The primary route for trade between Asia and Europe is via the Suez Canal. The Economic and Social Commission for Asia and the Pacific has identified three routes—Caucasus, Central Asian and the Caspian Sea route. The Corridor gives India access to Central Asian and Russian markets via Iran. Most importantly, the route bypasses Pakistan and Afghanistan.

In spite of high expectations, the Corridor is only partially functional. Speedy implementation of the INSTC is the need of the hour. There are many missing links in the project, which need to be resolved. In 2012, there was renewed interest among member countries to speed up the work on the Corridor. The sixth meeting of the Experts Group of the Coordination Council of the INSCT was held in May 2012 at New Delhi. It was proposed that 2 four-nation groups would be set up to address some of the outstanding issues of the project; the three original signatories-Iran, Russia and India will be part of both the groups.[19] Another suggestion that came up was the creation of a core group on customs to be based at New Delhi; it will comprise of experts from India, Iran, Russia and Turkey.[20]

In the last few years, the Turkmenistan-Afghanistan-Pakistan-India (TAPI) pipeline project has made some progress. It is welcoming to see Russia's positive response to the pipeline project. According to news reports, Putin as the Prime Minister had said that Russia is willing to "invest a half billion dollars in a power line from Tajikistan to Pakistan across Afghan territory and many more billions in a gas pipeline from Turkmenistan to India across Afghanistan and Pakistan".[21] If TAPI materialises, it would bring about a major change in the region by connecting South and Central Asia through a pipeline.

Another good model of India-Russia cooperation in the region could be the two countries jointly using the air base at Ayni in Tajikistan, which India has renovated. There were reports suggesting such a proposal but nothing official has yet come out. Rather than competing with each other, India and Russia can jointly use the base and set an example and help in reducing geo-political tensions in the region.

### *Afghanistan Angle*

India, Russia and CAS share similar concerns regarding the deteriorating situation in Afghanistan. These countries have been victims of threats emanating from Afghanistan: resurgence of Taliban, extremism, drug trafficking, etc. Central Asia (Uzbekistan, Tajikistan and Turkmenistan share borders with Afghanistan) as immediate neighbour of Afghanistan is most vulnerable to the developments in Afghanistan. For India and Russia too, an unstable Central Asia is detrimental to their national security.

India and Russia have in their official documents emphasised on resolving the crisis in Afghanistan. India's 'Connect Central Asia' Policy clearly states that India would strengthen 'strategic and security cooperation' with the CAS. The document states the key areas of cooperation as: 'military training, joint research, counter-terrorism coordination and close consultations on Afghanistan.'

Underlining the need for stability in Afghanistan, the 2013 Concept of the Foreign Policy of the Russian Federation mentions:

> "the ongoing crisis in Afghanistan and the forthcoming withdrawal of international military contingents from the country pose a great security threat to Russia and other CIS members. The Russian Federation together with Afghanistan and concerned countries, the United Nations, the CIS, the CSTO, the SCO and other multilateral institutions including Russia-NATO projects, will make consistent efforts to find a just and a lasting political solution to the problems faced by this country with due respect for the rights and interests of all its ethnic groups and achieve a post-conflict recovery of Afghanistan as a peace-loving sovereign neutral state with stable economy. Comprehensive measures to reduce terrorist threat from Afghanistan and eliminate or reduce illicit drug production and traffic in a significant and measurable manner will be an integral part of those efforts. Russia is committed to further intensifying international efforts under the auspices of the UN aimed at helping Afghanistan and its neighbouring states to meet these challenges".[22]

Afghanistan would be going through a double transition in 2014: the international forces leaving Afghanistan and the Presidential election. The increasing acts of violence, the menace of drug trafficking, the nexus between narcotics trade and extremist groups, political uncertainties and economic woes have worsened the security situation in the country.

The common thread binding the CAS, Russia and India is the desire to see a stable and a peaceful Afghanistan. Earlier too, these countries have cooperated with each other with regard to Afghanistan. For example, India has cooperated with Russia and CAS by supporting the Northern Alliance to fight the Taliban forces in Afghanistan.

The Central Asian countries are bilaterally engaged with Afghanistan in rebuilding the country. For example, during the period 2006-2009, Kazakhstan has given US$ 1 million humanitarian aid to Afghanistan, scholarships to several Afghan students to study in Kazakhstan, besides providing training to Afghanistan's police and internal security service, etc.[23] It is the only country in the region to have an Assistance Programme on Reconstruction of Afghanistan.[24] It has also built a school in Samangan province and a hospital in Bamiyan province.[25] Uzbekistan has been supplying power to Afghanistan since 2002 and has built bridges connecting Mazari-Shariff and Kabul, thereby linking the northern and eastern parts of Afghanistan.[26]

Bilateral relations between India and Afghanistan are deepening. In October 2011, India and Afghanistan signed the 'Strategic Partnership Agreement'. India was the first country with which Afghanistan signed such an agreement. India's engagement in Afghanistan is based on four broad areas—infrastructure projects, humanitarian assistance, small and community based development projects, and education and capacity development.[27] India's assistance is about US$ 2 billion, making it the fifth largest bilateral donor in Afghanistan,[28] as also the largest regional donor. Despite facing several attacks, India built the 218 km Zaranj-Delaram road connecting Iran to Afghanistan, which was inaugurated in January 2009. It also constructed the transmission line from Pul-e-Khumri to Kabul and helped build a substation at Chimtala, bringing Uzbek electricity to Kabul.[29] India is also constructing the Parliament building and the Salma Dam power project.[30]

Russia too is engaged in the reconstruction process of Afghanistan. Russian companies are engaged in the modernisation of the Naglu Hydropower Plant outside Kabul and for reviving the soviet type house-building factory in Kabul.[31] It has also expressed its willingness to reconstruct the Salang tunnel linking Kabul with the northern provinces.[32] The two countries have strong bilateral military cooperation and Russia has supplied spare parts for the military hardware the soviets left behind in Afghanistan, besides providing heavy armaments like tanks, helicopters and air carriers.[33] Russia is also engaged in imparting military training to Afghan military officers.

India, Russia and the CAS could take joint initiatives to rebuild the war ravaged Afghanistan. They could pool resources for bigger reconstruction projects to rebuild a new and strong Afghanistan. Regional players have been active in bringing together concerned parties, an example being the conference on Afghanistan held in Moscow in March 2009 under the aegis of the SCO. Another regional effort has been the quadripartite meetings involving Tajikistan, Pakistan, Afghanistan and Russia held twice in Dushanbe (2009 and 2011) and once in Sochi in 2010. The quadripartite meetings have not included India, so far. It would be worthwhile to consider India and other CAS to be included in the group for a greater regional participation. Here, Russia could take initiative to pave way for India's inclusion in the group.

## Conclusion

India-Russia cooperation in the Central Asian region will have deep geo-political implications. For any such cooperation to be fruitful, willingness and cooperation from the CAS is of utmost importance. It has been noted that "Russia and India have to focus on their cooperative engagement with Central Asia to deny any negative integration of the region at the cost of their own national interests as well as that of regional peace and stability".[34] India and Russia need to explore and nurture the avenues available for cooperation.[35] India-Russia cooperation on issues that are of common interest with respect to Central Asia is a positive indication to reduce unnecessary competition, and in the long run, might bring other countries with similar designs along with them.[36]

## NOTES

1. Ekaterina Koldunova. "Russia and India in Central Asia: Competition or Cooperation?". http://www.mgimo.ru/news/experts/document 131846.phtml (Accessed August 5, 2013).
2. The Ministry of Foreign Affairs of the Russian Federation."Concept of the Foreign Policy of the Russian Federation", 12 February 2013. http://www.mid.ru/bdomp/brp_4.nsf e78a48070f128a7b432569990 05bcbb3/76389fec168189ed44257b2e0039b16d!OpenDocument (Accessed May 1, 2013).
3. V.V. Naumkin *et al.*, "Russia's Interests in Central Asia: Contents, Perspectives, Limitations", Russian International Affairs Council (RIAC), No. 10, 2013.http://russiancouncil.ru/common/upload/RIAC_ Central_Asia_En.pdf (Accessed August 10, 2013).
4. Ajay Patnaik. "Central Asia in Indo-Russian Strategic Calculations", in P.L. Dash and Andrei M. Nazarkin (eds.) *Indo-Russian Diplomatic Relations: Sixty Years of Enduring Legacy* (New Delhi: Academic Excellence, 2008), pp. 152-153.
5. SCO was established as Shanghai 5 in 1996 and got its present nomenclature after Uzbekistan joined it as member in 2001. The group consists of six members—Russia, China, Kazakhstan, Kyrgyzstan, Tajikistan and Uzbekistan, five observers and three dialogue partners.
6. Address by Foreign Secretary at NDC on "Challenges in India's Foreign Policy", 19 November 2010. http://mea.gov.in/Speeches-Statements.htm?dtl/815/Address+by+Foreign+Secretary+at+NDC+on+Challenges+in+Indias+Foreign+Policy (Accessed April 12, 2013).
7. Angira Sen Sarma. "India's Membership of SCO: Present Scenario", Indian Council of World Affairs (ICWA), 7 January 2013. http://www.icwa.in/pdfs/VPIndiamembership.pdf (Accessed May 12, 2013).
8. *Ibid.*
9. Alexander Lukin. "Should the Shanghai Cooperation Organization be Enlarged?", 22 June 2011. http://eng.globalaffairs.ru/number/Should-the-Shanghai-Cooperation-Organization-Be-Enlarged—15245 (Accessed February 17, 2012).

10. Angira Sen Sarma, 2013, *op. cit.*
11. *Ibid.*
12. *Ibid.*
13. Angira Sen Sarma. "China's Growing Role in Central Asia", in M. Rasgotra (ed.) *Present Day China: A Net Assessment* (New Delhi: Academic Foundation, 2012), p. 147.
14. Ministry of External Affairs, Government of India. "Joint Statement furthering the India-Russia Strategic Partnership to meet the challenges of a changing World". http://www.mea.gov.in/bilateral-documents.htm?dtl/15701 Joint+Statement+furthering+ the+IndiaRussia+Strategic+Partnership+to+meet+the+challenges+of +a+changing+World (Accessed April 12, 2013).
15. Ministry of External Affairs, Government of India. "Keynote address by MOS Shri E. Ahamed at First India-Central Asia Dialogue", 12 June 2012. http://www.mea.gov.in/Speeches-Statements.htm?dtl/19791/Keynote+address+by+MOS+Shri+E+Ahamed+at+First+India Central+Asia+Dialogue (Accessed April 22, 2013).
16. Sandeep Dikshit. "India to Hold FTA Plus Talks with Customs Union Troika", *The Hindu*, New Delhi, 3 April 2013.
17. Angira Sen Sarma. *India and Central Asia: Redefining Energy and Trade Links* (New Delhi: Pentagon Press, 2010), pp. 80-90.
18. Later on Belarus, Kazakhstan, Tajikistan, Azerbaijan, Armenia, Syria, Oman, Turkey, Ukraine and Kyrgyzstan signed the agreement.
19. SandeepDikshit. "Despite U.S. Opposition, Iran to be Transport Hub for North South Corridor", *The Hindu*, New Delhi, 31 May 2012.
20. *Ibid.*
21. "Russia to Return to Afghanistan", 22 January 2011. http://voiceofrussia.com/2011/01/22/40804343/ (Accessed April 12, 2013).
22. The Ministry of Foreign Affairs of the Russian Federation, "Concept of the Foreign Policy of the Russian Federation", 12 February 2013, *op. cit.*
23. Embassy of the Republic of Kazakhstan in the United States. "Commitment to Assist Afghanistan". http://www.kazakhembus.com/index.php?page=foreign-policy (Accessed August 12, 2013).
24. *Ibid.*
25. *Ibid.*

26. ShoislamAkmalov. "Uzbekistan's Role in Stability and Development of Afghanistan", *Policy Perspectives*, vol. 6, no. 1, January-June 2009. http://www.ips.org.pk/international-relations/pakistan-and-its-neighbours/1048.html (Accessed July 20, 2013).
27. Ministry of External Affairs, Government of India. "India-Afghanistan Relations". http://www.mea.gov.in/Portal/ForeignRelation/afghanistan-aug-2012.pdf (Accessed May 1, 2013).
28. *Ibid.*
29. *Ibid.*
30. *Ibid.*
31. Bestuzhev Igor. "Afghan Army may Get Russian Helicopters", 31 January 2011. http://voiceofrussia.com/2011/01/31/42099769/ (Accessed April 10, 2013).
32. *Ibid.*
33. *Ibid.*
34. Ajay Patnaik. 2008, *op. cit.*, p. 158.
35. Angira Sen Sarma. "Indo-Russian Amity Mirrors on Central Asia's Advantage", in P.L. Dash and Andrei M. Nazarkin (eds.) *Indo-Russian Diplomatic Relations: Sixty Years of Enduring Legacy* (New Delhi: Academic Excellence, 2008), p. 551.
36. *Ibid.*

# 8
# India and Russia

## Redefining Engagement in the Asia-Pacific

*Pankaj Jha*

In the Asia-Pacific strategic discourses, the narrative from India and Russia is relatively constrained. Any policy articulation similar to US 'Asia Pivot' policy would be seen with apprehension. Russia will be perceived as revisiting its Cold War approach, while India will be seen as expanding its footprints in the region.[1] In order to dispel any such notion, their domestic discourses make repeated references about the priority given to their immediate neighbourhood[2] and the 'Near Abroad'.[3]

In the post 1990 liberalisation phase, India has been searching for markets and therefore enhanced its relations with developing and developed countries. During the same time, Russia burdened with inflation, unemployment and internal political dynamics had disengaged itself from the larger strategic space. However, the two countries are now slowly calibrating their future role in this region. This is partly driven by an incremental rise of India and a 'resurgent' Russia.[4]

The two countries have begun to project their benign posture.[5] This can be explained in terms of India's proactive approach to conciliate with its immediate and extended neighbourhood.[6] As a diplomatic move, India embarked on an active mission to address their concerns[7] while at the same time promoting its "Look East" Policy.

In the case of Russia, its withdrawal from Cam Ranh Bay, Vietnam signified its strategic retreat from the region. The Russian Ministry of Foreign Affairs (MFA) also gave the impression that major Asian countries were not as important as Russia's relations with the West.[8]

However in the first decade of the 21st century, there was a visible policy transition, when India and Russia began their engagement in multilateral institutions and extended neighbourhood[9] with much vigour. The catalyst in both the cases has been the shift in power dynamics from Europe to Asia and available resources at the disposal of both the countries. Further, the emergence and subsequent strengthening of new multilateral structures, primarily Shanghai Cooperation Organisation (2001), East Asia Summit (2005) and BRICs (2008) have catapulted these two nations as indispensable to the Asia-Pacific order. Russia's participation in Asia Pacific Economic Cooperation (APEC)[10] in 1998 in which India has not yet been granted membership (even though India was invited as an Observer in November 2011), showcased the different contours of engagement in the Asia-Pacific region.

In contrast, the membership configuration of the then Japanese Prime Minister Hatoyama East Asian Community[11] and Australian Prime Minister Kevin Rudd's Asia Pacific Community,[12] India figured prominently while Russia was excluded, clearly reflecting the preferences of the US allies. Nevertheless, when the issue of expansion of the East Asian Summit was discussed in November 2011, both Russia and the US were included in the extended EAS. By virtue of inclusion in EAS, the Russian representation was visible in the ASEAN Defence Ministers Meeting plus Dialogue Partners (ADMM+). This clearly shows that in terms of building consensus on regional security issue, Russia and India are seen as important players in the Asia-Pacific region. Perhaps what is important is how Russia and India can play constructive role in bringing about peace and harmony in the Asia-Pacific region.

## India and Russia Approach towards Asia-Pacific

During the "reforms" of the 1990s, Russia lost influence in East Asia and larger Asia-Pacific. Later, as Russia went forward and began to develop its economy, its activities in the region expanded. Indeed, the East Asian region started to play an increasing role in Russia's foreign policy. This can be attributed to the developments in Northeast Asia (primarily North Korea's nuclear ambitions) and developments in its eastern sea board. Russia's strategy in the region is aimed at maintaining the status quo and the balance between major powers. The Southeast Asian countries view China-centred regional cooperation as a model that could protect them from the influence of "hostile forces". They regard China's economic growth and prospective political umbrella as an opportunity for developing their own economies.[13] However, increasing Chinese assertive in East China Sea and South China Sea has invited the US attention in the region as well as triggered apprehensions about China's rise in the Asia-Pacific. The emergence of China in the regional strategic matrix further created a politico-strategic space for the two countries to manoeuvre in the region.

Russia has acted as a responsible member of international community, and this is articulated in its foreign policy statements. According to Russia's foreign policy priorities, all conflicts should be resolved on the basis of international law. In this regard, Russia's position is very clear and predictable. One of Moscow's main tasks is to build a constructive relationship with the United States, an extremely important component in preserving the equilibrium and balance of power and enhancing stability and security in East and Southeast Asia. The diversification of Russia's exports, which so far are limited mainly to raw materials, military-technical cooperation, and energy security issues, remains one of the most essentials tasks.[14] In order to achieve that Russia needs to expand and explore markets.

India also started building its constituency in the larger Asia-Pacific region through trade relationships/agreements with Thailand, Singapore, Korea, Malaysia, and Japan and has started negotiations with Australia, Indonesia and New Zealand. Also, India stead fastedly tried to create a fine balance between the US and China in its policy decisions.

Relations with the West continue to dominate Moscow's foreign policy; recent developments suggest that Russian policy makers are now reassessing the importance of the Asia Pacific region. The issues of "unilateral and illegitimate actions" as well as "disdain for international law" and "uncontained hyper use of force" were brought up by Vladimir Putin at the Munich Conference on Security Policy in February 2007, and his views are supported by many countries.[15] Taking a similar approach, Indian Prime Minister in its UN speech in 2011 rejected any external military intervention to settle domestic turmoil in any country.

Russia has actively engaged with its neighbours through multilateral cooperation and made efforts for economic integration. Last year, Moscow's new Pacific strategy was highlighted as Russia hosted the 2012 APEC Summit in its principal Pacific city, Vladivostok.[16] Russia is now a member of all the Asia Pacific multilateral security-focused and political bodies. Russia's preferred model for the Asia Pacific political order is a multi-polar system in which Moscow is one of the major players, along with Beijing, Washington, Tokyo, New Delhi, and perhaps Seoul and Jakarta[17]. Russia seems determined to change the fact that it remains one of the very few economies in the Asia Pacific not to have established any Free Trade Agreements (FTAs). In 2010, Russia launched formal negotiations with New Zealand, and FTAs with Vietnam and Singapore are currently being studied. It is also expected that Russia's accession to the WTO in December 2011 will help Moscow to advance its trade agenda in the Asia Pacific.[18] India also signed the India-ASEAN FTA and entered into negotiations on Services and Investment agreement with the multilateral organisation. It further showed its intent in joining APEC and initiated a series of initaitives to engage its Southeast Asia and Indian Ocean neighbours.

This clearly defines the role that the two countries have started outlining for themselves. Even though the approach has been different but the aim is to sustain their growth momentum through building better economic relations conducive for both national and regional development. However, there is a need to build consensus on larger economic integration and regional security.

## New Configurations and the Role of the Two Nations

Regional institutions like the Association of Southeast Asian Nations (ASEAN), ASEAN+3 (APT), the ASEAN Regional Forum (ARF) and the Asia-Pacific Economic Cooperation (APEC) have responded to new security challenges. As the regional institutional architecture changes, the key questions that need to be addressed are: (a) whether the current regional arrangements—now being referred to as akin to new, second-generation types of regionalism that are characteristically more robust and involve closer and wider forms of cooperation—are indeed able to mitigate the new attendant instabilities and security challenges facing the region; and (b) whether these new forms or layers of institutional arrangements allow for shifts in patterns of inter- and intrastate relations that bring with them new elite consensus on market regulation and dissemination of norms.[19] The multiplicity of security architectures and the need for better trade and investment relations have tried to influence each other in the larger scheme of things. With countries restricting supplies of critical raw materials in times of crisis or any regional tension, shows that scarce resources can act as decisive tools for exerting pressure. Few important suggestions have been made in a number of multilateral forums to build trust through economic complementarities. These are expanding the value addition network, building energy dependency through multi -nation energy pipelines and promoting micro regionalism based on sector specific arrangements. However, in order to achieve these, there is a need for building consensus on regional security so as to promote trade and investment.

## Emerging Challenges to the Regional Security and Economic Growth

Elucidating emerging challenges in the Asia Pacific, the Russian Foreign Minister has noted that:

> The issues at the agenda of Asia-Pacific Region (APR) today confirm the topicality of creating a secure system of interstate relations in the region. Its foundations must include the

> principle of indivisibility of security, non-admission of the attempts to ensure own security by harm to the security of other states, taking into account lawful concerns and interests of all parties. We are convinced that such model of security and cooperation needs to be built on out-of-block grounds, basing on supremacy of international law, equality, openness and inclusiveness.[20]

As is apparent, Russia has been carefully articulating its interests in the region and has shown keenness in participating in all initiatives including disaster risk reduction and collective efforts in countering Non-traditional security threats (NTS). However, the bigger question is how to bring convergence between economic priorities and security concerns, so as to promote economic growth and regional security. India and Russia can cooperate in this endeavour.

On its new Asia policy, Russia's Foreign Minister Sergey Lavrov has noted that Russia is not a newcomer in East Asia; Russia has enjoyed contacts with these countries since the 17th century, and played an important role in international relations in the region in the 19th and 20th centuries. Although this view might be disputed, one cannot deny the role of the Soviet Union in the victory of the national liberation movements in Asia.[21] A newly emerging concept of Russian geopolitical positioning being discussed at the moment argues that Russia is a Euro-Pacific power, which means it has both European and Asia-Pacific dimensions in geographical terms, but in terms of its political characteristics it is a European power.[22] Similarly, India also has been referring to the Asia-Pacific and the Indo-Pacific as its area of interest.

India and Russia are calibrating their strategic interests and protect their domestic industry while subscribing to the fundamentals of the World Trade Organisation; any dominance of any one particular economic structure would jeopardise their plans of incremental assimilation into international economic order. The two countries can work together on building consensus on economic and trade issues and also strategic thinking in the Asia-Pacific region.

## Conclusion

The regional security challenges in the Asia-Pacific region has defined the roles of the two countries. With Japan debating about developing its own military, North Korea becoming more unpredictable after its nuclear and missile tests, China's assertive behaviour in its eastern and south-eastern coast and the US using the 'Pivot Asia' strategy to engage willing players, the matrix is getting more vector dependent. With both independent and dependent variables working in this strategic matrix, a greater understanding between the two nations in the region would make better consensus building on both traditional and non-traditional issues.

Russia has adopted a more proactive and responsible attitude towards the regional issues while India has been adhering to its "strategic autonomy". As a result, the space and benefits for promoting cooperation is ever expanding. However, with both countries still nurturing apprehensions about the bilateral relations with China and the US, there is a need for a greater dialogue to rebuild understanding. Russia and India stand to gain by promoting peace and harmony in the larger Asia-Pacific region and can work as 'coolants' for maintaining the regional balance. For that, there is a need for concerted approach on developing a new thinking on integrating the region and promoting development.

## NOTES

1. David Scott. India's "Extended Neighbourhood Concept: Power Projection for a Rising Power", *India Review*, Vol. 8, no. 2 (April-June 2009), pp. 107-108.
2. Rajiv Sikri. *Challenge and Strategy Rethinking India's Foreign Policy*, Chapter 7 (New Delhi: Sage Publications, 2009). In fact, the concentric circles approach has been alluded to by the former Foreign Minister Pranab Mukherjee and also Shiv Shanker Menon, the National Security Adviser of India in a number of speeches.
3. The earliest use of the term was in Nexis, Fred Shapiro of New Haven writes, in an article in The Russian Press Digest of June 9, 1992, titled "Near Abroad Wants to Be Far". The term was meant to distinguish

new independent erstwhile Soviet republics form the Western nations. For further details see William Safire. On Language: The Near Abroad, *The New York Times*, May 22, 1994.Russia and the Near Abroad. http:/ /www.pearsonhighered.com/assets/hip/us/hip_us_pearsonhighered/ samplechapter/0205189938.pdf (Accessed August 8, 2013). Donald L. Berlin. India in The Indian Ocean, *Naval War College Review*, vol. 59, no. 2 (Spring 2006), p. 58. C.Rajamohan. India and Australia: Maritime Partners in the Indo-Pacific, *The Asialink Essays*, vol. 3, no. 6 (November 2011). http://www.asialink.unimelb.edu.au/__data/assets/ pdf_file/0008/505628/Maritime_Partners_in_the_Indo-Pacific.pdf (Accessed August 8,2013). For greater discussion about Near Abroad see Peter B. Humphrey, The State of Play in Russia's Near Abroad, Issue 55, 4th quarter (2009). http://www.ndu.edu/press/lib/images/ jfq-55/7.pdf (Accessed August 18, 2013).

4. Ivan Eland. Is a 'Resurgent' Russia a Threat to the United States? November 02, 2008. http://original.antiwar.com/eland/2008/11/01/ is-a-resurgent-russia-a-threat-to-the-united-states/ (Accessed August 20, 2013).
5. Frank G. Wisner II, Nicholas Platt, and Marshall M. Bouton. *New Priorities in South Asia: U.S. Policy Toward India, Pakistan, and Afghanistan,* Chairmen's Report of an Independent Task Force Cosponsored by the Council on Foreign Relations and the Asia Society (New York: November 2003), p. 3. Also see Dr. Madhavi Bhasin. India's Role in South Asia—Perceived Hegemony or Reluctant Leadership? http://www.globalindiafou ndation.org/MadhaviBhasin.pdf (Accessed August 9, 2013). Harsh V. Pant. India in the Indian Ocean: Growing Mismatch between Ambitions and Capabilities, Pacific Affairs: Vol. 82, No. 2 (Summer 2009), p. 281. William L. Dowdy, The Indian Ocean Region as Concept and Reality in William L Dowdy and Russell B Trood (ed.) *The Indian Ocean: Perspectives on a Strategic Arena* (New Delhi: Himalayan Books, 1987), p. 3. Arun Prakash. A vision of India's Maritime Power in the 21st Century, *Air Power Journal*, vol. 1, no. 2 (Winter Oct-Dec 2006), pp. 3-4. Commander Sarabjeet Singh Parmar. Maritime Dimension in India's National Strategy (Paper Presented in IDSA National Strategy Project Workshop, IDSA, New Delhi, December 20-23, 2010).
6. Carlyle A. Thayer. The Rise of China and India: Challenging or Reinforcing Southeast Asia's Autonomy? In Ashley J. Tellis, Travis Tanner, and Jessica Keough (Ed.), *Asia Responds to its Rising Powers:*

*China and India,* Strategic Asia 2011-12 (National Bureau of Asian Research, Washington DC, 2011), p. 312. Walter C. Ladwig. India and the Balance of Power in the Asia Pacific, no. 57, 2nd quarter 2010. http://www.ndu.edu/press/lib/images/jfq-57/ladwig.pdf (Accessed August 11, 2012). Also see Pankaj Jha. India and South Pacific - Multilateral Engagement, Bilateral Ties and Diasporic Connections (September 13-14, 2010, Asia New Zealand Foundation, Wellington, 2010).

7. India's intervention in Sri Lanka (1987-89) through Indian Peace Keeping Force (IPKF) and trade embargo on Nepal (1990) and military support to Maldives (Operation Cactus by Indian armed forces in 1988) during coup attempt were seen as India's hegemonic signatures.
8. Anna Kireeva. Russia's East Asia Policy: New Opportunities and Challenges. http://sam.gov.tr/wp-content/uploads/2013/03/3Anna_Kireeva.pdf (Accessed August 11, 2012).
9. David Scott. India's "Extended Neighborhood" Concept: Power Projection for a Rising Power, *India Review*, vol. 8, no. 2 (2009), pp. 107-143.
10. For a comprehensive debate on the Asia Pacific Multilateralism, kindly see John Ravenhill. The Numbers Game in Asia-Pacific Cooperation, in Christopher M Dent and Jorn Dosch (ed.) *The Asia-Pacific Regionalism and The Global system* (Cheltenham: Edward Elgar, 2012), p. 75.
11. John Hemmings. Understanding Hatoyama's East Asian Community idea (January 22nd, 2010) RUSI. http://www.eastasiaforum.org/2010/01/22/understanding-hatoyamas-east-asian-community-idea/ (Accessed August 11, 2012).
12. Carlyle A. Thayer. Kevin Rudd's multi-layered Asia Pacific Community initiative, June 22nd, 2009. http://www.eastasiaforum.org/2009/06/22/kevin-rudds-multi-layered-asia-pacific-community-initiative (Accessed August 11, 2012).
13. Vladimir N. Kolotov. Main Trends of Russia's Foreign Policy in Transforming East and Southeast Asia, April 2008. http://www.brookings.edu/research/opinions/2008/04/asia-kolotov (Accessed August 11, 2012).
14. *Ibid.*
15. *Ibid.*

16. Artyom Lukin. Russia looks to the Pacific in 2012, March 6, 2012. http://www.eastasiaforum.org/2012/03/06/russia-looks-to-the-pacific-in-2012/ (Accessed August 11, 2013).
17. *Ibid.*
18. *Ibid.*
19. Mely Caballero-Anthony. Non-traditional Security and Multilateralism in Asia: Reshaping the Contours of Regional Security Architecture? June 2007. http://www.stanleyfoundation.org/publications/pab/pab07mely.pdf (Accessed August 19, 2012).
20. Speech of Russian Foreign Minister Sergey Lavrov at the ministerial "retreat" of the 20th session of the ASEAN Regional Forum for security, Bandar Seri Begawan (2 July 2013). http://www.mid.ru/BDOMP//brp_4.nsf/english/B3BACB4BA3CF6F1F44257B9E00503410 (August 13, 2013).
21. Anna Kireeva. Russia's East Asia Policy: New Opportunities and Challenges. http://sam.gov.tr/wp-content/uploads/2013/03/3Anna_Kireeva.pdf (Accessed August 10, 2013)
22. *Ibid.*

# 9
# Russia and Pakistan Relationship
## Engagement after Estrangement

*Indrani Talukdar*

The bilateral relationship between Russia and Pakistan is growing at a remarkable pace. On May 1, 2013, the relationship marked the 65th anniversary between Russia and Pakistan.

Russia considers Pakistan an important country in the South Asian region as it has great economic potential. The country wants to increase bilateral trade and cooperation with Pakistan in diversified areas of economic activity. It is encouraging its Russian investors to invest in Pakistan for joint ventures and investment.[1]

### Russia-Pakistan Relationship: Inconsistent

Diplomatic relations between Russia and Pakistan can be traced back to May 1, 1948 when the relationship was first established.[2] At that time, there were a number of exchanges between the two countries to strengthen the relationship. The engagement has undergone many phases of ups and downs due to the changes in the international system. For instance, the bilateral relationship between Russia and Pakistan from the late 1940's till the 1970's was normal; however with the beginning of the Cold War, there was occasional discomfort between the two countries, mostly due to the growing alliance between Pakistan and the US.

In fact, three occasions can be highlighted to show the deterioration of Russia and Pakistan relationship. First occasion was during the 1971 India-Pakistan War when the then- Soviet Union supported India and the US supported Pakistan[3]; second was the 1979 invasion of Afghanistan by Soviet Union; and third was the India-Pakistan War of 1999[4]. In fact, the Afghanistan turmoil became the chessboard for the Cold War rivals, the US and Soviet Union, where Pakistan was an important supporter of the US and emerged as a conduit for the supply of arms and ammunition to the Mujahedeen. The Soviet leadership linked Pakistan with the Afghan struggle against the Soviet occupation. This resulted in a virtual 'state of war' between Islamabad with Moscow. Though the Soviet occupation ended in 1989, there was a general belief among the Russian political and military circles that Pakistan was responsible for forcing the Soviet Union out of Afghanistan.[5]

Nevertheless, when Soviets announced their exit from Afghanistan in 1987, Pakistan tried to downplay the tension with Russia by ensuring that the withdrawing Soviet troops were not harassed by the Mujahedeen. Pakistan also helped in facilitating contacts between the authorities in Moscow and the Mujahedeen groups for negotiating the release of some Russian Air Force personnel and other prisoners held by the Mujahedeen since 1985. This led to some improvement in bilateral relations.[6]

Meanwhile, with the end of the Cold War, Pakistan lost its status as a frontline state for the US, and Washington took a harder position on the nuclear issue. By October 1990, under the Pressler Amendment, it terminated military and economic assistance to Pakistan.[7] Although the cold shoulder given to Pakistan by the US gave rebirth to an improved Russia-Pakistan relations, but Russia's relationship with Pakistan was still measured.

During 1991, Russia continued to strengthen its strategic partnership with India more than Pakistan. The reasons behind this were Pakistan's hard financial crunch and the ban of military sales under the US Pressler Amendment of 1990. These two reasons made Pakistan's position weak in the international system and also for Russia. Apart from these rationales, there were other reasons for Russia's cautious approach towards Pakistan. Firstly, Pakistan's support to Islamic extremists groups which were helping the Chechnya's rebels against Russia and second, the ineffectiveness of Pakistan's narcotics control authorities in preventing the increasing smuggling of narcotics to Russia from Pakistan through the Central Asian Republics[8] that led to apprehensions in Russia to forge a stronger relationship with Pakistan.

Despite these inhibiting factors, Pakistan took the initiative in improving the bilateral relationship with Russia first under Prime Minister Benazir Bhutto (1994-1995) and later Nawaz Sharif in 1997[9] . After two years in power, Prime Minister Sharif visited Russia in 1999. During this period, both countries entered into a number of economic engagements (trade and industrial agreements). However, relationship between Russia and Pakistan degraded again. The reason for this degradation in the partnership was Pakistan's support to the Taliban regime in Afghanistan in 2001. During this disturbance in Afghanistan, Russia was supporting the opposing group, Northern Alliance group.

The event of 9/11 changed many relationships in the international arena, including Russia and Pakistan. Pakistan took the occasion to effectively transform the post-9/11 challenges into opportunities by adopting a proactive and pragmatic approach in its foreign relations. This approach helped Pakistan in staging a diplomatic comeback at regional and global levels. It understood the need to join the international effort of war against terrorism. This decision in countering terrorism consequently changed its policy towards the Taliban as well (covertly it still supports). Pakistan's initiative in countering terrorism helped in ushering a new era in the Russia-Pakistan relationship.[10]

From late 2001 onwards, a Russo-Pakistani rapprochement has been developing. In 2007, Kremlin sent its Prime Minister Mikhail Fradkov to Pakistan.[11] In response to this Russian initiative, President Asif Ali Zardari met with the Russian President Dmitry Medvedev for six times between 2008 to 2011. The bilateral engagement has been strengthened in trade and economy. Both governments at a trilateral meeting between Russia, Pakistan and UK held in London on February 2013 shared the trade figures between Russia and Pakistan for 2011 and 2012. The figure for 2011 was US$ 348 million and in 2012 it was US$ 570 million.[12] Both Russia and Pakistan is expecting an increase in the trade figures in the coming years.

## Reasons Behind Bilateral Cooperation

Russia and Pakistan has reasons for strengthening their partnership. Russia with its national interests and its need to modernize and strengthen its economy has to think of expanding its relationship with all countries including Pakistan.

## Russia's Rationale

Pakistan is strategically located with Punjab and Sindh province in its east, while Khyber Pakhtunkhwa forming the link to Afghanistan and Central Asia in the immediate west and Pakistan Occupied Kashmir (POK) in the north towards China. Balochistan on the other hand is linked to Iran, Turkey, Arabian Peninsula and Western Asia.[13] Russia feels that Pakistan's geo-strategic location will help the country in reasserting its role in its immediate sphere of influence and beyond. Russian President Vladimir Putin has shown willingness to adapt Russia's foreign policy to the new geopolitical realities through its multivectored approach in South Asia.

The strategies behind Russia's strengthening its engagement with Pakistan can be drawn from Russia's ambitions such as to gain a foothold in Central and South Asia; to have access to the warm waters that Pakistan's Gwadar Port can offer; and to make the US troops in Afghanistan directly dependent on Russia's logistics[14] apart from Pakistan's strategic location. Russia already controls the Northern Distribution Network in Uzbekistan and Tajikistan that border Afghanistan. If the southern routes from Karachi to Chaman and Torkham are added to this line of network distribution, then all deliveries will have to be coordinated through the Russian-Pakistani partnership.[15] Russia may feel that it will help in curtailing the US influence in this region.

The Gwadar Port holds crucial position for Russia like the rest of the world. Russia's gas giant Gazprom is reported to join the energy grid of Asia at Gwadar. In the future, the Russians and Central Asian states can link up with Gwadar via the north-south trade/energy corridor, a proposal which Pakistan may be willing to agree.[16] In fact, Gwadar will bind Pakistan, China, Russia and the Central Asian States together[17] and Russia through the Central Asian States will be able to use the seaport for trade and transit.

Meanwhile, Russian investors have expressed keen interest in the Thar Coalfield Project and the Central Asian and South Asian (CASA) project, which aims at establishing the necessary transmission and trading infrastructure to enable trade in electricity between Central and South Asia. Russia is also keen in investing in new projects through an offer to finance the refurbishment of the Guddu and Muzaffargarh power plants in Pakistan,[18] the Trans-Afghanistan Pipeline (TAPI) gas project, and the Iran-Pakistan (IP) gas pipeline project. Hence, there is convergence of the geo-economic interests of these two countries with their geo-strategic interests, which will help Russia and Pakistan to stabilize its economies which at present are weak.

Russia's interest in Pakistan can also be seen from the energy sector. Russia is an important oil and gas producer, preserving its status as a major transit country through which energy can be carried from the Caucasus and Central Asia to Europe. Energy is a tool of domestic modernization and international influence, which Russia is well aware of. In fact, Russia with its relationship with other key energy producers such as Pakistan can develop its capacity as a global middleman by coordinating its production with the rest of the key energy producers and offer its expertise in building energy infrastructure across the world.[19] This in turn will help Russia to strengthen its position and its economic condition.

Religion, apart from geo-strategic location, also plays an important role in the new world order. Russia and the world feel that Pakistan will be able to help in curbing Islamic extremism. The 26/11 event in India brought Pakistan in the forefront of international terrorism with the revelation of the country being a safe haven for the various Islamic terrorist groups. With the withdrawal of NATO's US-led International Security Assistance Force (ISAF) from Afghanistan in 2014, Russia fears that the state failure in Afghanistan will cause a spillover of Islamic fundamentalism into Central Asia, and from there into the southern regions of Russia.[20] Along with this, the narcotic issue like drug trafficking is of concern for Russia as it is affecting the Russian population. Hence, Russia needs Pakistan's assistance in controlling Muslim insurgents and narcotic trafficking.

### Pakistan's Rationale

Pakistan seeks to improve and have progressive relations with all countries and wants to dispel the impression of being a US proxy in the region. Although Pakistan and the US relationship has not deteriorated, there is some element of discomfort.

The US, after its invasion of Afghanistan in 2001, has conducted drone attacks in Pakistan to flush out terrorists in Pakistan's Federally Administered Tribal Areas (FATA) region. In 2011, Admiral Mike Mullen, the outgoing chairman of the Joint Chiefs of Staff, bitterly denounced Pakistani complicity in terror. He noted "in choosing to use violent extremism as an instrument of policy, the government of Pakistan—and most especially the Pakistani Army and ISI—jeopardizes not only the prospect of our strategic partnership, but also Pakistan's opportunity to be a respected nation with legitimate regional influence. By exporting violence, they have eroded their internal security and their position in the region."[21] Operation Neptune Spear of 2011 during which Osama bin Laden was killed in Abbotabad, Pakistan suffered another blow to its bilateral relationship with the US. The effect of this uncomfortable relationship can be seen in the form of US aid to Pakistan which has declined from US$ 1.9 billion in 2012 to US$ 1.2 billion for 2014.[22]

Meanwhile, Pakistan no longer sees US as a reliable and dependable partner because of latter's strong relationship with India. In fact, the strategy behind Pakistan's keenness in having a robust relation with Russia is to provide a strategic balance in the region vis-à-vis Indo-US rapprochement.[23] It also understands that partnership with Russia in the long run will help in upgrading its defence sector through security cooperation. In this context, Russia-Pakistan relationship is a two-way cumulative investment.

Pakistan is in need of military hardware and Russia can step in. At the same time, Pakistan can be a new market for Russian military hardware to keep its economy afloat[24] and also a prospective buyer.[25] A new seller-buyer relationship can be forged between Russia and Pakistan.

Efforts from both sides are on to expand defence ties and Russia and Pakistan are planning to strengthen this relationship by holding joint military exercises, exchanging trainees and trainers. Russian MI-17 helicopters currently form the backbone of Pakistan Army's logistics/troop lift capability and these can be upgraded to armed versions with Russian assistance. Both Pakistan and China seek to export the JF17 Thunder fighter jet which is powered by Russian engine and is jointly produced at Pakistan Aeronautical Complex, Kamra. In the long term, Kamra may witness Pak-China-Russia joint development/production of fighter aircraft under transfer of technology programme.[26]

## Implications on Russia-India Relationship

Hoes does this bolstering relationship between Russia and Pakistan concern India? Does it threaten the 'time-tested' partnership between Russia and India? Does India need to be cautious about it?

Russia and India celebrated its 66th anniversary of bilateral relationship on April 2013. Both countries have given credence to the strategic partnership. In the defence sector, Russia and India have moved from the traditional seller-buyer model with more advanced forms of close industrial cooperation integrating the two countries' scientific, resource and human potential. Russia supplies over 60 per cent of India's military hardware needs. Currently, Russia has about $7 billion (Rs. 35,000 crore) worth of defence contracts in India.[27] This showcases a robust relationship between India and Russia in this sector. However, India will need Russia's assistance in the upgradation of its defence system despite India diversifying its defence market to other countries; Russia will also need India for defence markets to sell its military hardware. Hence, both need each other for further cooperation in future.

Russia and India can cooperate in other areas of international politics and global issues as they both share common objectives and peaceful interests. In one of its latest reports, Russian International Affairs Council (RIAC) has ranked India next to the US and China in the world system. Russia believes that these three countries could shape world politics.[28] In the new Foreign Policy Concept of the Russian Federation, Russia has reiterated its desire to strengthen its relationship with India. Bilateral trade has grown steadily from US$ 7.5 billion (2009) to US$ 8.5 billion (2010), to US$ 8.9 billion (2011) and to US$ 11.04 billion (2012). During January-May 2013, the bilateral trade amounted to US$ 3.9 billion. India's exports to Russia amounted to US$ 1.3 billion while imports from Russia amounted to US$ 2.6 billion. The two-way investment between the two countries stands at approximately US$ 7.8 billion.[29]

Hence, the evolving relationship between Russia and Pakistan should not create much concern for India. However, India must keep itself abreast of the Russia-Pakistan developments and address its concerns with Russia at Track I and Track II deliberations if needed. India has to manoeuvre its way through the Russia-Pakistan relationship and strengthen its partnership with its 'time-tested', 'long standing' and 'special-privileged' relationship with Russia.

## Conclusion

The relationship between Russia and Pakistan is gaining momentum in the backdrop of post-2014 Afghanistan and the economic needs of both Russia and Pakistan.

In June 2013, Russian President Vladimir Putin at the St. Petersburg International Economic Forum put forth his intentions to 'take a page from the United States' book and pivot east'. He announced ambitious plans to boost Russia's economic growth by looking to the Asia-Pacific region rather than to its traditional markets in Europe.[30] Russia, undoubtedly, wants to regain its 'great power' status and wants to checkmate US influence in the Asia region, how much it will succeed remains questionable.

Russia may not be able to replace US in Pakistan and substitute it completely in the domain of defence collaboration, economic aid, trade and market for Pakistani goods. It is because there are certain realties that may be difficult to alter despite current situations. Today, US along with the European Union are the largest trading partners of Pakistan and their share in its economic development is too big to dispense with.[31]

For India, the country has to observe the relationship between Russia and Pakistan from close quarters. It is because the Russian deal is not limited to the defence system of India but also transcends to nuclear reactors, industries and space systems of India. If Pakistan manages to manoeuvre its way into the Russian military, industrial complex then it will be a major concern for India. Hence, India has to be cautious regarding the growing partnership between Russia and Pakistan.

## NOTES

1. "Russia wants to increase trade, commercial ties with Pakistan", *Daily Times*, August 25, 2013. http://www.dailytimes.com.pk/default.asp?page=2013%5C08%5C25%5Cstory_25-8-2013_pg5_14 (Accessed on August 26, 2013).
2. "Russia-Pakistan Relations", *Consulate General of the Russian Federation in Karachi*. (http://www.rusconsulkarachi.mid.ru/RUSSIA-PAKISTAN.htm Accessed on August 5, 2013)
3. Donaldson and Nocee. *The Foreign Policy of Russia*, p. 97, *op. cit.*
4. Russia vehemently criticized Pakistan for the 1999 Kargil war between India and Pakistan. "Pakistan-Russia Relations", *Wikipedia*. http://en.wikipedia.org/wiki/Pakistan%E2%80%93Russia_relations (Accessed on August 26, 2013).
5. Vijay Sakuja, "Will Russia Sell Military hardware to Pakistan? "*Unpublished Work*".
6. B. Raman. "Nawaz Sharif's Visit to Moscow", *South Asia Analysis Group*,

April, 15, 1999. http://www.southasiaanalysis.org/paper48 (Accessed on August 10, 2013).

7. Vijay Sakuja, *op. cit.*
8. Raman. "Nawaz Sharif's Visit", *op. cit.*
9. *Ibid.*
10. Muhammad Nawaz Khan and Beenish Altaf. "Pakistan-Russia Rapprochement and Current Geo-Politics", *IPRI Journal* XIII, no. 1 (Winter 2013), p. 126. http://www.ipripak.org/journal/winter%202013/std4.pdf (Accessed on August 9, 2013).
11. Sabir Shah. "A brief recap of the troubled Pak-Russia relationship", *The News*, October 4, 2012. http://www.thenews.com.pk/Todays-News-2-135657-A-brief-recap-of-the-troubled-Pak-Russia-relationship (Accessed on August 19, 2013).
12. *Sergey Kamenev. "Russia-Pakistan: the Way is Open for New Projects"*, Oriental Review, *February 12, 2013. http://orientalreview.org/2013/02/12/russia-pakistan-the-way-is-open-for-new-projects/* (Accessed on August 26, 2013).
13. Nadir Mir, "Pakistan-Russia geopolitics", *The Nation*, November 30, 2012. (http://www.nation.com.pk/pakistan-news-newspaper-daily-english-online/columns/30-Nov-2012/pakistan-russia-geopolitics Accessed on August 9, 2013).
14. Lyuba Lulko, "Pakistan can make Russia Queen of Asia", *Pravda.Ru*, August 28, 2012. http://english.pravda.ru/russia/politics/28-08-2012/122006-pakistan_russia-0/ (Accessed on August 5, 2013).
15. Rajashri Roy. "Russia and Pakistan New Equation", *IDSA Comment*, June 4, 2013. http://www.idsa.in/idsacomments/RussiaandPakistanNewEquation_rroy_040613 (Accessed on August 7, 2013).
16. Farooq Hameed Khan, "Pakistan-Russia: can old rivals be strategic partners?" *The News*, September 10, 2012. (http://www.thenews.com.pk/Todays-News-13-17390-Pakistan-Russia-can-old-rivals-be-strategic-partners, Accessed on August 10, 2013).
17. Mir, "Pakistan-Russia", *op. cit.*
18. *Sadhavi Chauhan. "Russia-Pakistan relations: beyond Putin's cancelled trip to Islamabad"*, Open Democracy, October 3, 2012. http://www.opendemocracy.net/sadhavi-chauhan/russia-pakistan-relations-beyond-putin%E2%80%99s-cancelled-trip-to-islamabad (Accessed on August 12, 2013).

19. Andrei P. Tsygankov, "Preserving Influence in a Changing World: Russia's Grand Strategy", *Problems of Post-Communism*, Vol. 58, No. 1, March-April, 2011, p. 7. (http://www.russiaotherpointsofview.com/2011/05/preserving-influence-in-a-changing-world-russias-grand-strategy.html Accessed on August 8, 2013).
20. Chauhan. "Russia-Pakistan relations", *op. cit.*
21. Rob Crilly. "Mike Mullen: Pakistan is 'exporting' terror", *The Telegraph*, September 22, 2011. http://www.telegraph.co.uk/news/worldnews/asia/pakistan/8783139/Mike-Mullen-Pakistan-is-exporting-terror.html (Accessed on August 13, 2013).
22. "US seeks sharp cut in aid to Pakistan: report", *The Nation*, July 4, 2013. http://www.nation.com.pk/pakistan-news-newspaper-daily-english-online/national/04-Jul-2013/us-seeks-sharp-cut-in-aid-to-pakistan-report (Accessed on August 13, 2013).
23. Nawaz Khan and Altaf. "Pakistan-Russia Rapprochement", p. 130, *op. cit.*
24. Russia's arms export business is declining. Ruslan Pukhov. "Arms Sales High, But Hard Times Loom", *The Moscow Times*, April 5, 2012. http://www.themoscowtimes.com/opinion/article/arms-sales-high-but-hard-times-loom/456173.html (Accessed on August 20, 2013).
25. Hameed Khan, "Pakistan-Russia", *op. cit.*
26. *Ibid.*
27. "Defence deals: Russia sees Red over India's tilt towards West", *Embassy of the Russian Federation in the Republic of India.* http://rusembassy.in/index.php?option=com_content&view=article&id=5713%3Adefence-deals-russia-sees-red-over-indias-tilt-towards-west&catid=16%3Apress-on-bilateral-relations&lang=en (Accessed on August 27, 2013).
28. Rajiv Bhatia. "Changing Russia a challenge for India," *The Tribune*, June 21, 2013.
29. "Bilateral Relations: India-Russia Relations", *Embassy of India*, July 2013. http://www.indianembassy.ru/index.php/bilateral-relations/bilateral-relations-india-russia (Accessed on August 13, 2013).
30. Fiona Hill and Bobo Lo, "Putin's Pivot: Why Russia is Looking East", *Brookings*, July 31, 2013. (http://www.brookings.edu/research/opinions/2013/07/31-russia-china-pacific-pivot-hill Accessed on August 6, 2013).
31. Nawaz Khan and Altaf. "Pakistan-Russia Rapprochement", p. 126, *op. cit.*

# APPENDIX I

## PM's Statement to the Media after the 14th India-Russia Annual Summit

21 October, 2013

Following is the text of the Prime Minister, Dr. Manmohan Singh's statement to the media after the 14th India-Russia Annual Summit today:

"I am very pleased to be back here in the historic and vibrant city of Moscow for the fourteenth bilateral Annual Summit.

At the outset, I would like to express my deepest appreciation to President Putin for his contribution in giving new direction and content to India-Russia relations as also for starting this very useful practice of Annual Summits between our two countries.

The depth, diversity and dynamism of our cooperation testifies to the fact that ours is truly a Special and Privileged Strategic Partnership. We also have a high degree of convergence on global developments and we collaborate constructively in international forums.

Our discussions today were characterised by the warmth, goodwill and trust that permeate all aspects of our partnership. President Putin and I agreed that our strategic partnership remains a matter of the highest priority for our two nations, based on our shared belief in the enduring value of this relationship, both for our mutual benefit and as a factor for global peace and stability.

We expressed satisfaction with the progress in our bilateral cooperation, including in defence, energy, high-technology trade, investment, space, science, education, culture and tourism. We noted that despite the fragile global economic environment, our bilateral trade grew by nearly 25% last year to reach 11 billion US dollars. We resolved to promote investments and facilitate closer cooperation in a number of areas with great potential, such as oil and gas, energy, information technology, telecommunications, pharmaceuticals, chemicals, fertilizers, and mining. I also sought President Putin's support for the launch of negotiations on a Free Trade Agreement with the Customs Union of Russia, Kazakhstan and Belarus.

The Kudankulam nuclear power project is an important symbol of our strategic partnership. We look forward to commercial power production from Unit 1 very shortly, and the completion of work on Unit 2 next year. I conveyed to President Putin our commitment to fully implement the road map on civil nuclear cooperation that was signed during his visit to India in 2010. We have directed our officials to resolve all outstanding issues at the earliest.

Our defence cooperation continues to be strong, and we expect that Russia will remain a key defence partner for India as we move into a stage of joint design, development, and production of key defence platforms.

We exchanged views on several major regional and global issues. India welcomes the joint Russia-US framework for the elimination of Syria's chemical weapons and I thanked President Putin for his personal efforts towards securing a peaceful political settlement to the Syrian conflict. India has a direct interest in peace and stability in the entire West Asian region. We also agreed on the need for a diplomatic solution to the Iranian nuclear issue and expressed hope for progress in the ongoing discussions with Iran.

India and Russia share similar perspectives on developments in our extended neighbourhood. Terrorism, extremism and drug trafficking emanating from this area endanger security and stability in our region and beyond. We have agreed to intensify our coordination and cooperation for promoting security and development in the region. We also emphasised our shared interest in a peaceful and stable transition in Afghanistan next year.

I congratulated President Putin on the successful conduct of the St. Petersburg G-20 Summit. Our two countries will continue to work closely together at various multilateral platforms, including the BRICS, the G-20, the East Asia Summit, and the United Nations.

Our people-to-people contacts remain strong. Between September and December 2013, ten Russian cities will host a festival of Indian culture. I believe that such activities will further cement the strong ties between our people.

The extraordinary history of our relationship and the warmth and goodwill between our peoples gives me great confidence that we will successfully exploit our growing convergence of interests and expanding opportunities for cooperation and take our strategic partnership to even greater heights. I thank President Putin for a very successful Summit."

# APPENDIX II

## Press Statement following Russian-Indian Talks

21 October, 2013

### PRESIDENT OF RUSSIA VLADIMIR PUTIN

"Ladies and gentlemen, Mr. Prime Minister,

Our talks have just ended. We discussed in detail the full range of our bilateral relations and outlined our next steps to continue strengthening the privileged strategic partnership between Russia and India.

Our countries and peoples are bound by traditionally strong ties of friendship, mutual respect and sympathy. This is the solid foundation upon which we are building our fruitful bilateral dialogue and are carrying out big projects in the economy, science and technology, and in humanitarian fields.

Our talks focused especially on economic cooperation. Despite the difficulties in the global economy, our bilateral trade increased by 24 percent last year. It is good to see that high-value-added products account for a big share of our trade. Engineering products account for half of Russia's exports to India.

Total Russian investment in India's economy is growing, as is Indian investment in the Russian economy. A large share of joint capital is being invested in projects in areas such as civil aircraft engineering, automotive industry, petrochemicals, telecommunications, pharmaceuticals, and fertiliser production.

Let me mention our biggest achievement too: in July, operations began at the Kudankulam nuclear power plant's first unit. It is being linked up to India's energy grid now, and indeed, I think this will happen literally in the next few hours. The second unit is in the works now, and there are plans for building more units, perhaps four more.

Russia's big companies are well represented on the Indian market. Gazprom, Power Machines, Stroytransgaz, SIBUR, KAMAZ, AFK Sistema and other companies are all working in India today. Dozens of Indian companies are also actively doing business in Russia.

We discussed our current military technical cooperation objectives. India is one of Russia's biggest partners in this area. Our joint projects in this sector are evidence of the high level of our technological and industrial cooperation. One of the biggest projects here is the modernisation of a heavy aircraft carrier, which will soon be ready to be delivered to India.

What distinguishes our military technical cooperation as it is developing now is the big share of research and development work we are carrying out. Russian and Indian specialists are working together on developing a fifth-generation fighter plane, a multipurpose transport plane, and missile technology.

Russia and India have always paid great attention to the common threat of terrorism and to its combat. We are doing all we can at national and international level and are joining forces to fight terrorism. We will do everything possible to prevent it and to make sure that perpetrators are punished.

In civilian cooperation fields, we are expanding our contacts in science and technology and in education. We hope that the science and technology cooperation programme that we approved today will help to further develop our ties in this area.

We remain just as keen as ever to develop our humanitarian ties too. The Indian Culture Festival is currently underway in Russia. We have decided to hold such events on a regular basis.

Of course, we also discussed current international issues. We work productively together in all of the international forums, including the UN, the G20, BRICS, and the Shanghai Cooperation Organisation.

We discussed in depth the situation in the Middle East, North Africa, and above all, in Syria. We exchanged information on our views on the situation in Afghanistan too. I want to note that our assessments are identical or very close on all of these issues.

We on the Russian side are happy with today's talks. They were successful and I am sure that they will help us to continue developing the multifaceted cooperation between our two countries.

I want to thank the prime minister of India, Mr Singh, and all of our Indian friends and colleagues.

We have big cooperation plans and I am sure that they will be carried out. Thank you."

# APPENDIX III

## Joint Statement of the 14th India-Russia Annual Summit: "Deepening the Strategic Partnership for Global Peace and Stability"

21 October, 2013

1. The Prime Minister of the Republic of India, H.E. Dr. Manmohan Singh, paid an official visit to the Russian Federation on 20-22 October 2013, at the invitation of the President of the Russian Federation H.E. Mr. Vladimir V. Putin. President of the Russian Federation, H.E. Mr. Vladimir V. Putin and Prime Minister of India, H.E. Dr. Manmohan Singh held talks in Moscow.
2. The President of the Russian Federation and the Prime Minister of India welcomed the continuing momentum of high-level bilateral contacts and intense dialogues that had taken place during the year, between the National Security Councils, the Foreign Offices and the various Ministries and Departments of the two countries. They discussed priority areas of bilateral cooperation and noted common positions on current international and regional issues. Both sides stressed their continued commitment to promote and strengthen in every possible way their special and privileged strategic partnership.
3. The sides noted a number of productive visits held this year at ministerial level to promote bilateral cooperation. These included the visits to Russia of H.E. Mr. S Khurshid, External Affairs Minister (in April and October, 2013), H.E. Mr. S K Shinde, Home Minister (in April, 2013), H.E. Mr. A Sharma, Minister of Commerce & Industry (in April, June and September, 2013), and H.E. Mr. P Chidambaram, Finance Minister (in July 2013).
4. The sides welcomed the enhanced bilateral parliamentary exchanges and particularly, the visit by Chairperson of the Federation Council of the Russian Federation Ms. Valentina I. Matvienko to India in February, 2013.

**Promoting Trade and Investment Ties**

5. The sides expressed satisfaction at the record level of bilateral trade of over US $ 11 billion reached in 2012.
6. The sides agreed that investment collaboration was an important component of economic cooperation, which could also help in increasing bilateral investment and trade. They welcomed the identification of priority investment projects on both sides as an outcome of the first meeting of the India-Russia Working Group on Priority Investment Projects. They noted the successful outcomes of the 2nd session of India-Russia Working Group on Modernization and Industrial Cooperation held in Moscow, where both sides acknowledged their mutual desire to further strengthen bilateral cooperation in areas like civil aviation; chemical and fertilizer industry; mining; and automobiles.
7. The sides welcomed increasing business interactions, as demonstrated by the successful traditional round table "Russia-India Business Dialogue" organized in the framework of the 17th Saint Petersburg International Economic Forum on June 20, 2013, and the seventh India-Russia Forum on Trade and Investment, also held in St. Petersburg, on September 20, 2013. They also welcomed the two meetings in 2013 of the reconstituted Chief Executive Officers Council, which was working out sectors and opportunities for greater business cooperation.
8. The sides underlined the significant potential for cooperation in such sectors as oil and gas, pharmaceutical and medical industry, infrastructure, mining, automobiles, fertilizers, aviation, as well as in modernization of industrial facilities located in the two countries.
9. The sides stressed the importance of the India-Russia Inter-Governmental Commission on trade, economic, scientific, technical and cultural cooperation (IGC) functioning as a key mechanism for developing bilateral interaction in the economic and investment fields. They noted the positive outcomes of the nineteenth session of the IGC held in Moscow on October 4, 2013.

10. The sides agreed to work towards the creation of a Joint Study Group for studying the possibility of signing a Comprehensive Economic Cooperation Agreement (CECA) between India and the Customs Union of Belarus, Kazakhstan and the Russian Federation. They noted that this matter was currently under the consideration of the Eurasian Economic Commission.

**Energy Cooperation**

11. The sides reaffirmed their commitment to implement the Agreement between the Government of the Russian Federation and the Government of the Republic of India on the Enhancement of Cooperation in Oil and Gas Sector concluded on December 21, 2010.
12. The sides noted the importance of cooperation in order to organize long-term supplies of hydrocarbons to India from Russia, conducive to strengthening India's energy security and diversification of energy exports from Russia through LNG supplies to India. The sides expressed satisfaction with the dynamic development of cooperation between JSC Gazprom and Indian companies to organize long term supplies of LNG to India from the Gazprom Group portfolio.
13. Both sides also agreed to explore the possibilities of direct transportation of hydrocarbons from Russia to India through the land route. The sides agreed to set up a Joint Study Group in this regard.
14. The Indian side expressed OVL's interest in participating along with Russian companies in exploration for hydrocarbons in the Arctic region.
15. The sides welcomed the signing of the Memorandum of Understanding on Energy Efficiency between FSBO Russian Energy Agency of the Ministry of Energy of Russia and the Bureau of Energy Efficiency of India.
16. The sides noted with satisfaction the progress in regard to the commissioning of Unit-1 of the Kudankulam Nuclear Power Plant and agreed to take necessary steps to expedite the completion of Unit-2. The sides also agreed to expeditiously finalise the General Framework Agreement and the Techno-

Commercial Offer for Units- 3 & 4 of the Kudankulam Nuclear Power Plant. The sides reaffirmed their commitment to the Agreement between the Government of the Republic of India and the Government of the Russian Federation on cooperation in the construction of additional nuclear power plant units at Kudankulam site as well as in the construction of Russian designed Nuclear Power Plants at new sites in the Republic of India, concluded on December 5, 2008; the Agreement between the Government of the Republic of India and the Government of the Russian Federation on Cooperation in the use of Atomic Energy for Peaceful Purposes and the Road Map for the Serial Construction of the Russian designed Nuclear Power Plants in the Republic of India, concluded on March 12, 2010.

17. The sides emphasized the need to facilitate cooperation among power sector companies of both the countries for modernization of existing power plants and construction of new power plants in India.
18. The sides expressed satisfaction with the signing of the Vladivostok Ministerial Declaration and Plan of Action on Regional Cooperation for Enhanced Energy Security and the Sustainable Use of Energy in Asia and the Pacific, 2014-18.

**Cooperation in Science and Technology**

19. The sides noted with satisfaction progress in various on-going scientific sectors, including cooperation in Basic Sciences under DST-RFBR program and the Integrated Long-Term Program (ILTP).
20. The sides welcomed the creation of new institutional mechanisms by the Ministry of Education and Science of the Russian Federation and the Ministry of Science and Technology of India. These mechanisms would support Indo-Russian R&D projects with potential for technology development and generation of new intellectual property. These projects would be in conformity with national priorities of both countries, as identified under 12th Five Year plan of India and the Federal Targeted Programme "Research and Development in Priority

Fields of Science and Technology Complex of Russia in 2014-2020".

**Education Sector Cooperation**

21. The sides agreed to expedite finalization of the intergovernmental agreements on recognition of education documents and academic degrees in the general and the medical fields of study. They noted the constructive discussion in Moscow in October 2013 on the issue of medical degrees.

**Cultural Cooperation**

22. Both countries, possessing a rich cultural heritage and guided by the centuries-old traditions of friendship, agreed to make extensive use of each other's culture and arts, and the mutual lively interest in these. The sides expressed satisfaction at the ongoing implementation of the Cultural Exchange Program 2013-2015 between the Ministry of Culture of the Republic of India and the Ministry of Culture of the Russian Federation, signed on December 24, 2012. They favoured further cooperation in the field of culture and the arts, including interaction between the major museums of both the countries.
23. Both sides commended the high level of goodwill and mutual appreciation of culture at the people-to people level. They welcomed the increasing people-to-people contacts between the two countries, including the flow of tourists, which increased by over 20 percent in each of the past two years.
24. The sides appreciated the organisation of the Festival of Russian Culture in India in 2012 and the ongoing Festival of Indian Culture in Russiain 2013. They also agreed tocontinue holding regular Russian cultural festivals in India and Indian cultural festivals in Russia.

**Inter-Regional Cooperation**

25. The sides recalled the Agreement for Cooperation between States and Regions of India and Russia (2000) and expressed

support for enhancing exchanges between regions of both countries. The leaders also encouraged city-to-city/sister-cities cooperation with a view to promote multifaceted engagement in economy, culture, health, education and public policy at a sub-regional level between the two countries.

**Exploration of Outer Space**

26. The sides expressed their commitment to further cooperation in space activities of mutual interest.
27. The sides supported cooperation between Russia and India within the UN Committee on the Peaceful Uses of Outer Space and agreed to advance it in a pragmatic and steady manner. In particular, they expressed mutual interest in coordinating actions with reference to the current endeavour of the Committee to work out guidelines related to ensuring the long-term sustainability of outer space activities.

**Military and Technical Cooperation**

28. The sides emphasized that the traditionally close military and technical cooperation between the two countries was a crucial element of the strategic partnership and reflected the high level of trust between the two states.
29. In the context of the 13th meeting of the Russian-Indian Inter-Governmental Commission on Military-Technical Cooperation scheduled in Moscow later this year, the sides commended regular bilateral contacts and military and technical cooperation, as well as the joint INDRA exercise conducted by the Armies of the two countries in October 2013. The sides emphasised the scope for enhancing service-to-service exchanges, training cooperation and regular exercises between their armed forces.
30. The sides welcomed the delivery of the Russian-built frigate Trikand to India in 2013, licensed production of Su-30MKI aircraft and T-90S tanks in India, as well as successful completion of the trials of the aircraft carrier Vikramaditya. The sides took note of the progress made in the field of joint design, development and production of high-technology

military equipment and implementation of projects such as the construction of the fifth-generation fighter aircraft, multi-role transport aircraft and BrahMos supersonic missile. The sides agreed to enhance cooperation in the fields of rocket, missile and navaltechnologies and weapon systems.

**Coordination on International and Regional Issues**

31. The sides re-affirmed their desire to build a more stable, secure and fair system of international relations based on equal partnerships between states, the rule of international law and respect for the purposes and principles of the UN Charter. They agreed to continue interaction with a view to strengthening the central role of the UN in maintaining international peace and security and ensuring steady social and economic development. The sides welcomed the scope of their cooperation within the UN and agreed to further coordinate approaches on a broad range of international and regional issues.
32. Both sides reaffirmed the need for UN Security Council reform in order to make it more representative and effective in dealing with emerging challenges. They agreed that any expansion of the Security Council should reflect contemporary realities. In this regard, the Russian Federation reiterated its strong support to India for a permanent seat in a reformed UN Security Council.

**Combating Terrorism**

33. The sides recalled the Moscow Declaration between the Russian Federation and the Republic of India on International Terrorism signed on 6 November 2001 and reiterated that international terrorism is a threat to peace and security and a grave violation of human rights and a crime against humanity. Both sides affirmed the need to join efforts of all states to defeat terrorism. They condemned terrorism in all its forms and manifestations and agreed that there should be no tolerance for sheltering, arming, training, or financing of terrorists.
34. In multi-ethnic and democratic societies such as India and the Russian Federation, terrorist acts perpetrated under misleading slogans are in reality attacks on the freedom and democratic

values of our societies and are aimed at undermining the territorial integrity of our nations. Such acts may have international linkages extending across and beyond the borders. States that provide aid, abetment and shelter for such terrorist activities are themselves as guilty as the actual perpetrators of terrorism.

35. Both sides reaffirmed the obligation of all states to vanquish terrorism from their territories and areas under their control. They need to irreversibly shut down terrorist networks, organizations and infrastructure, and show tangible movement in investigating and bringing quickly to justice all those responsible for acts of terrorism.
36. Both countries further agreed that there cannot be ideological, religious, political, racial, ethnic, or any other justification to acts of terrorism. Incidents such as the Mumbai Terror Attacks or Beslan terrorist attack, which resulted in the death of numerous innocent civilians cannot be justified on any grounds.
37. The sides reaffirmed the UN's central role in combating international terrorism, and expressed their intention to make an active contribution to counter terrorism under the auspices of the UN. They also called for a speedy conclusion of the negotiations on the draft UN Comprehensive Convention on International Terrorism. The sides also agreed to continue to address these issues in the format of the bilateral Joint Working Group on Countering International Terrorism.

**International Information Security**

38. The sides expressed concern at the growing threat of the use of information and communication technologies for criminal and terrorist purposes, as well as for purposes that are inconsistent with the UN Charter. In this context the sides noted the need for adoption by the international community of the universal rules, norms and principles of responsible behaviour of states in the use of Information and Communication Technologies. They agreed to deepen their bilateral consultations and cooperation on global issues related to the use of Information and Communication Technologies. They also decided to accelerate consideration of the proposed intergovernmental

agreement on cooperation in the field of international information security. The sides also stressed the necessity to observe the principle of non-interference in internal affairs as well as human rights in Internet, including the right to privacy, in accordance with respective domestic legislation.

**Cooperation in the field of Disarmament and Non-proliferation**

39. Russia and India consider as their common task preventing proliferation of weapons of mass destruction and their delivery means. They emphasized the importance of step-by-step progress in the field of disarmament with the participation of all stakeholders to uphold international peace, security and stability.
40. The sides welcomed the bilateral consultations on Arms Control and Non-Proliferation which were held in New Delhi in May this year and gave the opportunity to exchange views on a whole range of topical issues. They agreed to strengthen multilateral export control regimes as important components of the global non-proliferation regime.Russia took into positive consideration India's interest in full membership in MTCR and Wassenaar Arrangement. The Russian side reiterated readiness to assist and promote a discussion and positive decision in the Nuclear Suppliers Group on India's full membership in the NSG, and welcomed India's intention to seek full membership. Indiastressed its determination to actively contribute to the international efforts aimed at strengthening the nuclear non-proliferation regime.
41. While recognizing the unalienable right of all states to use nuclear energy for peaceful purposes Russia and India stressed the need for countries to comply with their respective non-proliferation obligations. The sides advocate the central role of the IAEA, and in particular its safeguards system, in the international activities aimed at the usage of nuclear energy for peaceful purposes in accordance with the requirements of the respective legally-binding safeguards obligations of states and the Statute of this organization.
42. Both sides support international efforts to ensure that outer space is used for peaceful purposes. Both legal instruments and

appropriate and inclusive confidence-building measures can contribute to this end.

**Enhancing Security Cooperation in Asia and the Asia Pacific**

43. The sides noted that the role of the Asia-Pacific region in international affairs is on the rise and supported further regional integration and cooperation for sustainable global growth.
44. The sides agreed to closely interact in order to discuss the framework principles of strengthening security cooperation in the Asia-Pacific region, based on universally accepted principles and norms of international law, openness, transparency and equality. They agreed to play an active role in multilateral for a to encourage further dialogue on equal and undiminished security and developing mutually beneficial cooperation in the Asia-Pacific region, in accordance with the agreement achieved at the East Asia Summit (EAS) held on 9-10 October 2013 in Brunei Darussalam.
45. The sides consider the EAS a key forum for strategic dialogue between leaders of member states on pressing issues as to the political and economic cooperation in the Asia-Pacific region.
46. The sides agreed that the Shanghai Cooperation Organization (SCO) contributed significantly to ensuring peace and stability, economic development and prosperity in Eurasia. The Russian Federation commended India's active participation in the SCO as an observer state and reiterated its strong support for India's bid for full membership of the SCO.
47. The sides are committed to further intensifying political interactions between China, India, and Russia. In this context, they attach great significance to the next meeting of the Ministers of Foreign Affairs of the three states, which is to take place this November in New Delhi. The sides also see it as essential to continue consultations concerning regional security at the level of High Representatives of China, India, and Russia.
48. The sides noted the role of Asia-Pacific Economic Cooperation forum (APEC) as an important mechanism aimed at creating favourable conditions for trade and investment cooperation and developing regional integration in the Asia-Pacific. Russia reaffirmed that India's potential membership in APEC would

facilitate further development of a dialogue on addressing key issues of regional and global trade. Russia reiterated its support towards India's accession to APEC upon achievement of consensus within APEC on expansion of its membership.

49. The sides expressed committed to further strengthening the ASEAN Regional Forum, a key tool for practical cooperation in maintaining peace and stability in the Asia-Pacific region, to increasing its contribution to the global effort to combat terrorism and cross-border crime, including in the field of ICTs. The sides voiced their intention to promote further development of multilateral military cooperation in the region, to coordinate measures and provide, on a mutual basis, support within the ASEAN Defence Ministers Meeting Plus (ADMM-Plus format).

50. The sides reaffirmed their commitment to further advance, in order to ensure peace, stability and prosperity in the Asia-Pacific region, cooperation and coordination within the interstate associations existing in the region, including the Asia-Europe Meeting Forum, Conference on Interaction and Confidence-Building Measures in Asia, Asia Cooperation Dialogue.

**Cooperation among BRICS countries**

51. India and Russia appreciated the outcome of the Fifth BRICS Summit in Durban (held on March 27, 2013). They noted the increased role which BRICS played in the efforts of the international community aimed at bringing the world economy to the path of strong, sustainable and balanced growth. India and Russia stand for strengthening of BRICS as a mechanism for a strategic and ongoing coordination of the activities undertaken by the member states on a growing range of international political and economic issues.

52. The sides confirmed their full support for the eThekwini Action Plan adopted at the BRICS Summit in 2013 and expressed determination to contribute actively to its implementation.

53. India and Russia stressed the importance of developing all aspects of multilateral cooperation within BRICS as the most solid basis for further strengthening of diverse ties among its members. The countries support the projects for establishing

the BRICS Development Bank and the Contingent Reserve Arrangement among BRICS states. The Indian side agreed to consider the Russian proposal to develop a Strategy of Multilateral Economic Cooperation of BRICS member states. The sides expressed confidence that the forthcoming BRICS summit in Brazil will help strengthen the role of BRICS on theinternational stage.

**Situation in Syria**

54. The sides expressed the strong belief that the crisis in Syria should not be resolved by force, and could be settled only through political means. Both countries expressed support for the early convening of an "International Conference on Syria" (Geneva-II), to take forward the Geneva-I Communiqué adopted in June 2012, which will bring all parties to the conflict to the negotiating table. The Indian side commended Russia's role in working towards a diplomatic solution to the Syrian conflict. The Russian side stated that it would welcome India's participation in Geneva– II. Russia and India support the process of placing Syria's chemical weapons under international control and their destruction in accordance with the decision of the Organisation for the Prohibition of Chemical Weapons (OPCW) of 27 September 2013 and the provisions of the Chemical Weapons Convention; the UN Security Council Resolution of 2118 is pertinent in this regard.

**Stabilization of the Situation in Afghanistan**

55. The sides approved the efforts made by the Islamic Republic of Afghanistan to begin an Afghan-led dialogue on reconciliation with the armed opposition forces, provided that these groups should respect the principles adopted by the international community, namely, to recognise the Constitution of the Islamic Republic of Afghanistan, to renounce violence and to sever ties with Al-Qaeda and other terrorist organizations. The sides considered it necessary to extend the sanctions regime introduced by the UN Security Council against the Taliban as one of the most important tools for fighting terrorism.

56. The sides were pleased to note that there was a growing understanding in the world of the essential role played by the states neighbouring the Islamic Republic of Afghanistan as well as by the countries and organizations in the region. The sides strongly called for the development and improvement of interaction within the existing frameworks of regional cooperation, such as the Shanghai Cooperation Organization (SCO), the Collective Security Treaty Organization (CSTO), the South Asian Association for Regional Cooperation (SAARC) and dialogue within RIC and the Istanbul Process.

57. The sides recognized terrorism as the major threat to Afghanistan's security and stability that jeopardizes peace in the region and in the whole world. Therefore they stressed the regional aspects of terrorism and extremism, emphasizing the necessity of joint and coordinated efforts and cooperation between the states of the region, especially taking into account the expected drawdown of international forces in 2014, in order to combat terrorism in all its forms and manifestations, including elimination of terrorist safe havens and cutting off financial support to terrorism.

58. The sides expressed concern about the scale of illicit drug production in Afghanistan and underlined that revenue from drug trafficking were one of the main sources of financing terrorist organizations. The sides agreed to continue taking effective measures to combat illicit drug trafficking of Afghan origin and to focus on permanent and active support for the Paris Pact initiative.

**Iranian Nuclear Program**

59. The sides expressed concern about the situation around Iran and its nuclear program. They confirmed their support for a comprehensive and permanent settlement of this situation, through political and diplomatic means, by establishing a dialogue. They recognize Iran's right to continue using nuclear energy for peaceful purposes in accordance with its international obligations. The sides urged Iran to comply with the provisions

of the corresponding resolutions of the UN Security Council and cooperate with the IAEA.

## Multilateral Economic Cooperation and Financial Reforms

60. The sides stated that there were still numerous challenges relating to the growth of the world economy. They considered it necessary to boost multilateral cooperation in order to tackle these. They attach particular importance to the G20 as the primary forum for international economic cooperation. India highly appreciated the Russian G20 Presidency as well as the outcomes of the Saint Petersburg G20 Summit. They stressed that the continuous implementation of its recommendations with respect to the decisions aimed at speeding up world economic growth, midterm fiscal consolidation, higher employment, liberalization of trade and promoting development will facilitate the solution of the key global economic issues. Russia expressed gratitude to India for the significant contribution towards success of the Saint Petersburg Summit.
61. Russia and India stressed the necessity to create a more representative and legitimate international financial architecture. They agreed that the primary task in this connection was to complete the Fifteenth General Review of IMF Quotas not later than in January 2014.
62. The two sides stressed that the G20 policy coordination process needs to pay more attention to monetary policy in the reserve country currencies in order to protect the international financial system and to prevent destabilization of financial markets.

## Environment and Sustainable Development

63. The sides welcomed the outcome of the UN Conference on Sustainable Development "Rio+20" (held in Rio de Janeiro, Brazil, on June 20-22, 2012) and stated that it was necessary to work consistently to implement its decisions. They attached great importance to addressing purposefully the global climate change problem and stressed the importance of boosting international efforts aimed at drafting a new

comprehensive and balanced climate change agreement by 2015.

64. The India-Russia Annual Summit was held in an atmosphere of traditional friendship and mutual understanding. The Prime Minister of the Republic of India expressed gratitude to the leaders of the Russian Federation for the hospitality and warm welcome in Moscow and invited the President of the Russian Federation to India. The invitation was accepted with pleasure.

# Index